The Da Vinci Code
and the
Secrets of the Temple

Robin Griffith-Jones

The Master of the Temple

CANTERBURY
PRESS
Norwich

© Robin Griffith-Jones 2006

First published in 2006 by the Canterbury Press Norwich
(a publishing imprint of Hymns Ancient & Modern
Limited, a registered charity)
9–17 St Alban's Place,
London N1 0NX

www.scm-canterburypress.co.uk

Reprinted 2006

British Library Cataloguing in Publication data

A catalogue record for this book is available
from the British Library

ISBN 1-85311-731-5
978-1-85311-731-2

Typeset by Regent Typesetting, London
Printed and bound by
Bookmarque, Croydon, Surrey

Contents

This book is based on my talk on *The Da Vinci Code*, given regularly in the Temple Church in London. A video of this talk is available at <u>www.beliefnet.com</u>.

Robin Griffith-Jones
Master of the Temple

List of Topics

You may want to refer straight away to particular questions raised by *The Da Vinci Code*. Here is a short list of the pages in this book at which they are discussed.

Foreword

Mid-morning, on an ordinary weekday, here at the Temple Church in London. Time for Brian, the verger, to open the church for visitors. As usual, there are several waiting to come in; at least one will be carrying *The Da Vinci Code*. Brian already knows what they will ask: 'Where are the knights' effigies?' 'Where is the knight's tomb lacking an orb?' And most eagerly of all, '*Have you read the book?*'

Brian still insists on believing – or pretending to believe! – that they are asking about the Bible.

I am writing this in my house next to the Temple Church. I am the 'Master of the Temple'. In the thirteenth century the Master of the Temple was one of the most powerful men in England. He was the monk who ran the order called the Knights Templar in England: the Templars' conspicuous courage in battle – and their fabulous wealth – made them a force to be reckoned with.

Those were the days. I have inherited the Master's title, but none of his power. (In *The Da Vinci Code*, the Master's name is the Reverend Harvey Knowles. An altar-boy weighs up the pros and cons of breaking the Church's normal rules: 'The altar-boy hesitated, well acquainted with Mr Knowles' . . . foul temper when anything cast this time-honoured shrine in anything but favourable light.' I hope I do not bear too close a resemblance to my fictional counterpart!)

Robert Langdon, Sophie Neveu and Sir Leigh Teabing – the three principal characters in the novel – are on their search for the Holy Grail. They have been following clue after clue. Now they are looking for a knight's tomb apparently without an 'orb' that should be on it. Their search has brought them to the Temple Church.

Pursuing the trio, by secret arrangement with Teabing, are his manservant Rémy and the giant albino Silas, a monk and member of Opus Dei. First Silas confronts the trio here in the 'Round Church', the oldest and most mysterious part of the building. The plan goes awry. Rémy breaks cover, gun in hand. He threatens to shoot his own master Teabing, if Robert will not hand over the vital cylinder. What can Robert do? He gives Rémy the cryptex. The clues to the Holy Grail are now in the hands of its most determined enemies.

Next stop, Westminster Abbey (with a quick murder in between). The pace is rising, as the book reaches its climax. No wonder the Temple Church has become a destination for Dan Brown devotees.

It has been a pleasure to welcome to the Temple the many visitors who have been enthralled by the novel and want to see its locations for themselves. I have been giving a weekly talk about the book; every week there are members of the audience who ask important questions with a genuine interest. I enjoy hearing these questions, and hope that I have been able to address most of them. This short book is an extended version of that talk. Over and again Dan Brown comes very close to something deep and important – and then veers off, at the last moment, on a tangent into pure fiction. You may well be wondering, as many of our visitors do, how much in *The Da Vinci Code* is true. It is a good question – and deserves a real answer.

This is not the first book to have been written about *The Da Vinci Code*, and will probably not be the last. I am sometimes asked why I have taken the trouble to write it. Do I really think the novel is that important? – I would like to rephrase the question: Do I really think the novel's *readers* are that important, and the questions they ask? Yes, I do. I would gladly have taken twice the trouble and written twice as much, if it would have helped. But you may be glad to have in your hand a short book which covers a fair amount of ground.

It's as well I let you know from the outset: this is a quite different book from those others beside it on the bookshop shelves. Everything depends, in any account of the past or present, on the angles from which they are lit and the viewpoint from which they are seen. Dan Brown gives us tantalizing glimpses of Opus Dei, the Last Supper, the Templars and the Gnostics: enough, among the shadows, for us to be gripped by their mysteries. It's time to draw back the veil and to see them all more fully in a brighter light. Will this destroy their mystique? On the contrary. Their real stories are just as exciting and moving and often just as baffling. There are heroes and villains here (and villains disguised as heroes!); there are fervour, ambition, rivalry, betrayal and love. I am about to set off on a journey back through time: through 2,000 dramatic years of Christian history. I hope you will enjoy coming with me.

Part 1
The Da Vinci Code

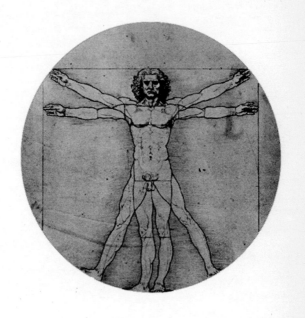

I

Everyone Loves a Conspiracy: The Gospel According to Dan Brown

'Everyone loves a conspiracy,' says the librarian in *The Da Vinci Code*. She is right, and in the novel we have conspiracy and counter-conspiracy, woven through the history of Europe for 2,000 years. At the heart of the story is the Roman Catholic Church: misogynist, oppressive and dishonest to the core. The plot of *The Da Vinci Code* turns on one great secret, forever suppressed by the Church: Jesus and Mary Magdalene were married. But the Church, according to the book's characters, has been hiding more than just a fact. For the celibate men wielding power in the Church have always feared and hated the whole principle that Mary Magdalene represents: the Sacred Feminine.

Let's start with the historical claims made in *The Da Vinci Code*. Are some or all of them true? We begin to think they might be. All the churches deny them, of course, not just the Roman Catholic Church. That's hardly surprising. The claims are chiefly about the world's churches, their power and the lies their power is based on. For centuries the celibate men in charge of the churches belittled women and warned against the sexual pleasure that women can enjoy and share with men. Why should we believe church leaders now – most of them men, many of them celibates – when they decry Dan Brown?

How strange it is, say church leaders, that so many readers cannot tell fact from fiction: the facts told in the Bible, from the fiction told by Dan Brown. But we all know that the churches themselves cannot agree what in the Bible itself is fact and what is fiction. Why should we respect the churches' views about Dan Brown when those churches cannot agree about their own Bible?

We can see why they are having trouble. The theory on which *The Da Vinci Code* is based was set out at length in the 1980s book *The Holy Blood and the Holy Grail*, co-authored by three writers. One of them, Henry Lincoln, was challenged about his book's claims. They were surely incredible? Lincoln replied: 'Is it more plausible that a man should be married and have children, or that he should be born of a virgin, attended by choirs of angels, walk on water and rise from the grave?'

It is a perfectly sensible question. Why should we believe the bizarre stories about Jesus? It is, for a good many of us, not enough to be told we must believe what is in the Bible by churches whose power and wealth depend on our believing that the Bible is true.

Faced with the success of *The Da Vinci Code*, Cardinal Bertone of Genoa in Italy has joined the fray. The book, he says, 'aims to discredit the Church and its history through gross and absurd manipulations. You can find that book everywhere and the risk is that many people who read it believe that those fairy tales are real. I think I have the responsibility to clear things up: to unmask the cheap lies contained in books like that.'

Of course, if we choose to take the Cardinal's word for it, the issue is closed. But *The Da Vinci Code*, if it aims to discredit anything, aims to discredit cardinals. The Cardinal may be right in everything he says, but his interests are obviously served in saying it. He is using his position to urge Catholic bookshops not to sell the book and Catholic readers not to read it. This *sounds* like the Catholic Church trying to suppress a book that is so popular because it tells us how ruthlessly the Catholic Church suppresses books.

How much of what we read in the novel is true, how much is plausible, how much is fanciful? We will start by telling the story of Christendom as told to Sophie by Teabing and Robert. We will then move backwards through history from the twentieth century to the first, picking out some of the moments and movements that matter most for the plot of *The Da Vinci Code* – and for anyone with an interest in the history that has made our world what it is today.

2

Jesus, Sex and the Church:
Two Thousand Years of Lies?

Here is the history of Christendom as relayed by
Robert and Teabing:

Jesus was a man; he knew well the value of women,
men and sexual relations between them. So he should.
For he was married to Mary Magdalene; they had a
daughter, Sarah. Mary Magdalene and Sarah eventually escaped from persecution in the Middle East and
reached France. Sarah had descendants of her own,
and these became the family of the Merovingian kings
of France. The blood-line is still flowing: there are
descendants of Jesus alive in France and Scotland
today – and so, no doubt, in the various countries
in which the French and the Scots have settled. You
yourself, the reader, may be a descendant of Jesus and
Mary Magdalene.

Jesus died. His male followers resented and resisted
the influence of Mary Magdalene. It was all too easy,
in a man's world, for these men to take control of the
followers that Jesus left behind. As the generations
passed, a movement gathered strength among these
followers towards celibate, monastic life. Jesus him-

self, in retrospect, was reinvented as a celibate; all record of his marriage was suppressed.

Celibate men were now running the emergent churches. Such men had ample reason to keep women well away from themselves, physically; and ample excuse, therefore, to keep women well away too from the power that men enjoyed. Women were sidelined, belittled – and worse. How had Eve tempted Adam? She had *seduced* him. Sin and death had entered the world through sex; and in particular through the sexual power of women. As Eve had been a fatal danger to Adam, so were all the daughters of Eve now portrayed as a danger to all the sons of Adam.

In 312 CE the Roman Emperor Constantine converted to Christianity. He gave the faith his imperial favour, and within a few years declared Jesus to be God. And so the married man Jesus had finally, nearly 300 years after his death, been transformed not only into the celibate Jesus but into God himself.

Those who knew the truth about the married Jesus were forced out of the mainstream churches. They retreated to the deserts of Egypt. In the late 1940s a cache of long-lost texts was discovered there, telling of Jesus. He suddenly took on the contours of a real man again. These texts, written in the second or third centuries after his death, tell how Jesus loved Mary Magdalene more than any of his other followers; he would often kiss her, and entrusted secrets to her and her alone – a privilege deeply resented (as these texts make clear) by the male disciples.

But as Sarah's descendants survive, so does the secret about their great ancestor, Jesus himself. At the time of the crusades, this secret was preserved by two societies. One was the Order of the Knights Templar. The Templars' task was, ostensibly, to protect pilgrims on their journeys in the Holy Land. This in itself attracted huge wealth and power to the order. But the knights discovered as well, in their headquarters on the Temple Mount in Jerusalem, some *proof* that Jesus and Mary Magdalene had been married. This gave the Templars unlimited power over the kings and popes of Europe. For if they once revealed to the world this secret of the married Jesus, the Templars would bring the churches' faith, their power and their wealth to an end.

What, then, was the other society involved with the family of Jesus? The Priory of Sion. The Priory actually protected Sarah's descendants from the attacks of the Church; and does so to this day.

The Priory of Sion keeps itself to itself, but among its Grand Masters have been some of the most famous artists and thinkers of all time. In the plot of *The Da Vinci Code*, one Master stands out above all: Leonardo da Vinci. *The Last Supper*, painted in Milan, is his masterpiece. Hidden within its composition is a clue to the Priory's secret. For the figure next to Jesus at the table, joined to him at the hip and wearing clothes the colour of Jesus' clothes, is not one of Jesus' male disciples at all; *it is Mary Magdalene, the wife of Jesus*.

The Roman Catholic Church, through the centuries, has had a careful and sometimes murderous eye on the Priory. No organization is better equipped to fight the Priory than the most loyal, devout and wealthy sect within the Church: the worldwide semi-secret society, Opus Dei. For as long as the Priory makes no move to reveal the secret about the married Jesus, the Church will at worst wage a low-level war of attrition against it. But if the Priory ever threatens to speak out, Opus Dei will respond. Ruthlessly.

This is quite a story. Whatever we finally make of it, it is exciting and immensely interesting. Of course the churches may respond angrily; they may say we have no right to invent the Jesus we want; that we gain nothing except a fantasy, if we do; and that, if we want to know about Jesus, we should go to the Bible and the churches' teaching. But this is disingenuous. Every generation has depicted the Jesus which that generation has needed: the Emperor, the liege-lord, the philosopher, the political radical, or the gentle Jesus, meek and mild. Our generation is doing the same: depicting the Jesus we need. But in our day, for the first time in centuries, the churches cannot control the portrait. Jesus is still an ideal figure for many of us: an example of how we should live our own lives. Such an exemplar will surely have made and honoured the greatest commitment one person can make to another: he will have been married. Those who suggest that Jesus was married are not belittling either Jesus or marriage; nor are they succumbing to a modern obsession with sex. They are trying to give to marriage and to sex within marriage the ultimate excellence which the Roman Catholic Church still gives only to 'consecrated celibacy'.

The marriage that is imagined here is modern:

marriage in which man and woman regard themselves and each other as equal partners, freed from all the patriarchal assumptions with which history – and the churches – have burdened it. It is marriage, too, in which sexual fulfilment is celebrated, happily and without qualification. Such a marriage between Jesus and Mary Magdalene is imagined as history, but a richly symbolic history. For in this marriage the Female is freed from subjection and from shame, and stands alongside the Male – Christ himself – as his equal and partner.

A fulfilling sexual relationship can clearly engender a hopeful, purposeful, confident commitment to a partner; and, in many cases, it may well be that this hope, purpose, confidence and commitment would all be diminished if the relationship were starved of its sexual element. That is, sex is about far more than sex. The churches have degraded it, through past centuries, by locating human sexual urges among our lowest instincts. The churches of today have little right to lament the results of that degradation for which the churches of times past are in good part responsible. Those who ask if Jesus was married are not aiming to contaminate Jesus with sex, but to free sexual life from the contamination the churches have found in it.

In the account of Robert Langdon and Leigh Teabing, the whole story of Jesus has been disguised and distorted by his followers for nearly 2,000 years. On this plot of lies, cover-up and silence the whole Christian Church is built. But there is a counter-plot. A handful of people, in each generation, has kept safe from harm the documents and the family that can show up the churches' lies for what they are. One day these people will disclose the truth. By its disclosure all Christendom will be overturned. The world will be freed from the grip of the patriarchal Church. And the way will be open at last for men and women to live as they should live: as equals in life, love and power.

Power: it can sound so crude to label the relations between men and women in such terms. We may find it more awkward still to ignore the churches' evident good will and good works and to analyse instead their leaders' longing for power. But it is a theme running like a scarlet thread right through *The Da Vinci Code*. So let's listen to one final protest, such as we might hear from the novel's readers who do actively distrust the churches.

Whenever the churches are weak, they praise the virtues of weakness (in the name of the suffering Jesus); but their leaders always have an eye on power – and the moment they get it, they claim divine authority (in the name of the kingly Christ) for all the bullying use they put it to. It can be immensely heartening to hear of a Jesus who broke free, in his own lifetime, from the constraints, corruption and complacency of institutional religion. As he had broken free, so (we sometimes hear) did his true followers. These faithful few promoted self-knowledge without interference from a self-appointed and self-serving priesthood. They defied the leaders of powerful churches that colluded ever more deeply with the governments of the day. No wonder they were forced outwards to the fringes of the churches and of the Roman Empire alike. But they still appeal today to those of us who refuse to submit to the arrogance of churches that have simply lost all sight of their founder, his life and his ideals.

Have you ever felt this way about Jesus, marriage and the churches, or known others who have? If so, then you or they may well have found *The Da Vinci Code* really heartening: the welcome disclosure, cast as fiction, of some very unwelcome truths.

But how much of that story, told by Robert and Teabing, is likely to be true? Let's start with the twentieth century, and move steadily backwards towards Jesus himself – and Mary Magdalene. I will simply be offering vignettes of a few moments and movements in Christian history: those of greatest importance for the plot of the novel. Dan Brown has chosen well; he has stirred into his brew some of the most dramatic periods and people in the history of Europe. But he has, bizarrely, mixed in as well a tiny society led by a fraudster. It is with this that we start.

Part 2
'Fact' – or Fiction?
The Priory of Sion and
Opus Dei

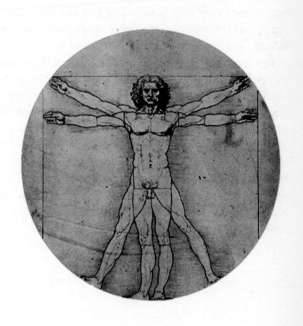

3

Ancient or Modern?
The Priory of Sion

The Priory of Sion was founded in the 1950s by the Frenchman Pierre Plantard in Annemasse, a town in Haute-Savoie in the South of France.

Plantard had been involved before World War Two with right-wing organizations dedicated to the recovery of monarchical, chivalric, Roman Catholic France. It is hard to imagine that he was an attractive character. During the war he set up a monthly newspaper 'for a Young Knighthood', which praised the Vichy government and denounced 'the corrupt principles of the old Jewish-Masonic democracy'. After the War he was imprisoned for fraud and embezzlement. On his release he renewed the promotion of his social and political agenda, and founded the Priory of Sion. Its secondary name (and the title of its magazine) was CIRCUIT, spelling out the initials of *Chevalerie d'Institution et Règle Catholique d'Union Indépendante et Traditionaliste*, 'Knighthood, of Catholic Institution and Rule, of Independent and Traditionalist Union'.

Plantard named the Priory after the hill 'Mont Sion'

close to Annemasse; it was only in retrospect that he saw the advantage in claiming a connection with Mount Sion in Jerusalem. During the crusades the canons of the Abbey of Our Lady of Sion, on the edge of Jerusalem, had been one of several groups guarding the city's holy sites.

You may remember that at the start of *The Da Vinci Code* Dan Brown declares some facts on which the novel's plot is based. Among them is the following: 'The Priory of Sion – a European secret society founded in 1099 – is a real organization. In 1975 Paris's Bibliothèque Nationale discovered parchments known as Les Dossiers Secrets, identifying numerous members of the Priory of Sion.'

But this is not a fact after all. Plantard claimed that he himself was the rightful heir of the kings of France. To press his claims, he and his associates *deposited* in the Bibliothèque Nationale a cache of *printed* documents to which they themselves gave the title *Dossiers Secrets*. Parchments? No. The documents are typed and printed; they cannot possibly antedate the invention of the typewriter.

The *Dossiers* came to fame thanks to the TV-journalist and producer Henry Lincoln. He made a trio of documentaries for the BBC, and with two colleagues – Michael Baigent and Richard Leigh – wrote a bestseller, *The Holy Blood and the Holy Grail*. They found link after link between Plantard and the mysterious story of Rennes-le-Château, near Mount Bezu in south-west France: its priest in the 1880s, the Curé Saunière, was said to have found ancient parchments and vast treasures. Describing their research into the *Dossiers*, the three authors seem excited by the game being played out for their benefit. In *The Holy Blood and the Holy Grail* we read: 'Periodically some of the individual pages [of the *Dossiers*] would be removed. At different times other pages would be freshly inserted. On certain pages additions and corrections would sometimes be made in a minuscule longhand. At a later date, these pages would be replaced by new ones, printed and incorporating all previous emendations.'

Just once or twice, during their research, the scales nearly fall from their eyes. They realize that one document could have been doctored to work a very effective hoax; and, they write, 'at times we nearly dismissed the whole affair as an elaborate joke, a hoax of extravagant proportions'. But instead they watched themselves, quite blithely, being used: 'There appeared to us only one plausible motivation for such a procedure – to attract public attention to certain matters, to establish credibility, to engender interest.' Yes, precisely: to attract public attention through the credulity of these authors themselves.

In Plantard's early publications there had been no word, it seems, about the mysteries surrounding Rennes-le-Château, its priest Saunière, its parchments and its treasures (the elements that play so large a part in *The Holy Blood and the Holy Grail*). It was in the 1960s that Plantard discovered how closely that local mystery tied in with the claims he was trying to establish for himself; and in the *Dossiers Secrets* he and his associates wove these themes into a single fantasy.

So was it all a joke? Not quite. Plantard – with his

'discreetly aristocratic bearing', 'gently amused indul-
gent twinkle', 'imposing authority' and criminal
record as a con-man – was glad to persuade people
that he was the heir to the throne of France; and these
authors were just what he needed. But a hoax? Yes.
And once the journalists were fooled, they were on
course to fool the world.

Some readers of *The Da Vinci Code* have felt
slightly cheated when they discover that Dan Brown,
like so many others, was taken in by the story of the
Secret Dossiers. But perhaps we would do better
simply to enjoy its bizarre contortions. Dan Brown
does. His story starts with the death of the curator
Saunière, named after the Curé Saunière at Rennes.
His villain is Sir Leigh Teabing, a fusion of two names
made famous by *The Holy Blood and the Holy Grail*:
the authors Leigh and (in anagram) Baigent. His
policeman is Bezu Fache, named after Mount Bezu
near Rennes; Fache is endlessly – and appropriately –
angry, *fâché*.

Two sets of facts are declared on the frontispage of
The Da Vinci Code. One is about the Priory of Sion,
the other about Opus Dei. It's time to turn to the
second of these; and from a web of fantasy to the solid
world of facts.

4

Opus Dei: Where Did It All Start?

'Opus Dei', declares Dan Brown on his frontispage, 'is a deeply devout Catholic sect that has been the topic of recent controversy due to reports of brain-washing, coercion and a dangerous practice known as "corporal mortification".' In the novel, two members play major roles: Bishop Aringarosa, frantic to save Opus Dei from danger; and the albino monk Silas, utterly loyal to Opus and to the Bishop, his saviour and patron. Aringarosa schemes ruthlessly with all the vast wealth at Opus' command for its preservation and its power. Silas has been brainwashed into torturing himself and, at his Teacher's command, into murdering others. Money, power, secrecy and a cult-like control of the members – so are these really the hallmarks of Opus Dei?

Ask any members of Opus Dei if this sums up their society, and they will (I suspect) stare at you in disbelief. They will say it is so wide of the mark that any response must start from scratch, and along the following lines: Opus Dei exists to support its members in a distinctive vocation – a personal, intimate call from God to place their whole life at his service in the world. Members of Opus Dei are committed to bringing Christ to their ordinary life and work, and to bearing witness to Christ in every day's ordinary occupations. For all work and all daily life has a spiritual meaning and it is up to each one of us to discover it; it is not necessary to withdraw from the world – in any 'religious' way – to find God. Each baptized Christian is free to reach Christ in the way that he or she feels called to undertake; and each such Christian is personally responsible for his or her decisions. Such decisions can be hard to take and hard to live up to; but God is our Father and we need not fear anything from the world. *That* is what Opus Dei is about.

It will be as well to bear in mind, through the next couple of chapters, this summary of Opus Dei. We are about to uncover the organization's foundations; we will then be able to make sense of everything built on top of them.

I wonder if you find this summary, as I do, both rather inspiring (I am, after all, a Christian minister!) and rather confusing. Confusing for two reasons. First, these insights and ideals are not specific to Opus Dei – a great many Protestant ministers in England or America would have claimed them, for hundreds of years, as the insights and ideals they promote among their people. And second, the summary makes no mention of those insights and ideals that *do* seem to be, except in monasteries, specific to Opus Dei. Let's hear of some of those insights and ideals in the words of the founder of Opus himself, the Spanish priest Josemaría Escrivá.

I quote from *The Way*, Escrivá's book of 999

maxims that has been translated into over 30 lan-
guages. Several million copies have been sold; it
remains Escrivá's classic, and an inspiration to Opus'
members. A Spanish bishop wrote the Preface to the
first edition, published in 1939. 'Reader,' he urged,
'do not rest; always stay alert and vigilant, because
the enemy does not sleep. If you make these maxims
your life, you will be a perfect imitator of Jesus Christ
and a gentleman without blemish. And with Christs
like you, Spain will return to the old grandeur of its
saints, wise men and heroes.'

The following extracts cannot, of course, do justice
to the book as a whole. I have selected just a few
themes and bunched their maxims together. I hope
that this will bring out some of the book's accents
clearly: the emphases on leadership, celibacy, obedience, unity, fixed purpose (there is little room here for
withdrawal to another form of life!) and the priesthood.

Give in? Be just commonplace? You, a sheep-like
follower? You were born to be a leader! (16) Be
firm! Be strong! Be a man! And then . . . Be an angel!
(22). If they see you weaken – you, the leader, it is
no wonder their obedience wavers (383). Leaders!
Strengthen your will so that God will make a leader
of you (833).

A priest – whoever he may be – is always another
Christ (66). To love God and not to revere the priest
– this is not possible (74). The prayer most pleasing
to God is the prayer of priests and consecrated
virgins (98).

Marriage is for the rank and file, not for the officers of Christ's army (28). The soul and body are two enemies that cannot be separated, and two friends that cannot get along (195). Treat your body with charity – but with no more charity than you would show towards a treacherous enemy (226). It is among the chaste that the most clean-cut men from every point of view are found. And among the impure abound the timid, the selfish, the hypocritical and the cruel – all characters of little manliness (124). Let your prayer be manly; to be a child does not mean to be effeminate (888).

Patriotic fervour – which is praiseworthy – leads many men to give their lives in service, even in a 'crusade'. Don't forget that Christ too has 'crusaders' (905). Don't worry if people say you have too much *esprit de corps*. What do they want? A delicate instrument that breaks to pieces the moment it is grasped? (381). Let's not forget: unity is a symptom of life; disunion is decay, a sure sign of being a corpse (940). Obedience, the sure way. Blind obedience to your superior, the way of sanctity (941). Unity. Unity and submission. What do I want with the loose parts of a clock – even though they are finely wrought – if they can't tell the time? (962). When a layman sets himself up as an arbiter of morals, he frequently errs; laymen can only be disciples (61). A director: you need one, in order to offer yourself, to surrender yourself, by obedience (62).

'There are so many ways!' you told me dejectedly.
There need to be many, so that each soul can find its
own way in that wonderful variety. Bewildered?
Make your choice once and for all; and the confusion will turn into certainty (964). Convince
yourself that for you – yours is the only way (965).

Have you heard stories about former members of
Opus who had felt they were being 'brainwashed' or
under enormous pressure not to leave the society?
How easily the society's devoted members, boldly
applying those maxims of Escrivá, could come to
hurt people, already confused, who had chosen the
route of Opus and only found themselves in even
deeper confusion.

We need to find a viewpoint from which we can see
the development of Opus Dei, from its foundation in
Spain in the 1920s through to the present day. Why?
Because the broad river of today's organization is still
shaped and fed by the waters of that first small spring.
The landscape through which it flows has changed
vastly, but the river – although far wider and deeper –
is recognizably the same river it was, nearly 80 years
ago.

Think of Spain, and what comes to mind? Sun-
baked beaches, siestas, fiestas, flamenco – and the
Roman Catholic Church. Surely Spain is the most
devout, conservative Catholic country in Europe?
Well, this is only half the story. The Church has for
centuries been loved and hated in equal measure for
the role it has had in Spanish society. As early as 1838

a newspaper could insist that the clergy were there 'to inspire the obedience of the masses towards the classification of society. It is essential that religion teach people that without obedience there is no society.' Any social problem could be resolved through charity, with 'the voice of the clergy counselling the wealthy'. How would such a Church face the tumultuous changes that were already transforming the economies and politics of Europe?

By the 1920s, Spain was in political turmoil. The Church's overt – and conservative – political affiliations were adding fuel to the flames of anticlerical resentment. The Jesuits, a religious order founded in Spain in the sixteenth century, offered a different approach. They had long held a dominant role in Spanish education; they cannily picked out their most talented students and nurtured them in the Jesuits' own Marian Congregations. The Vatican recommended that the Jesuits' policy be more broadly applied: the Spanish Church should form ostensibly *non-political* organizations, promoting the reconstruction of a Christian social order. The Jesuits themselves ran a newspaper, *Reason and Faith*. A Jesuit, Angel Herrera, edited the Catholic daily *El Debate* and in 1908–09 helped found an organization avowedly for Catholic newspapermen, the *Asociación Católica Nacional de Propagandistas* (ACNP). The ACNP had grand ambitions: to advance a few select Catholic university students capable of playing a role in public affairs. 'Education and the press', said Herrera in 1925, 'are the two great enemy fortresses.' Herrera insisted that the ACNP was apolitical; and indeed it was, inasmuch as it was not a political party. But it was to play a leading and very public role in the polity of Spain. Herrera himself hoped it would mobilize a 'directing minority' to lead the country away from decadent liberalism and prevent a putsch by either extreme, Left or Right.

Watching the country's deepening crises was the young priest, Josemaría Escrivá. He had trained in Saragossa, and knew its Cardinal Soldevila well. Saragossa was a stronghold of the most radical Left, which endorses terrorism; in 1923 Cardinal Soldevila, advocate of a strong line against social extremism, was assassinated there. Escrivá was ordained in 1925, then moved to Madrid to study for a doctorate in civil law; he worked at the school of journalism that produced Herrera's newspaper, *El Debate*. Madrid's university was as bitterly polarized as the rest of Spain. The atheist, anti-monarchist Left was working to secure positions of influence there through the *Institución Libre de Enseñanza*. The Catholic Association of Students, by contrast, was attracting little support.

Escrivá derided the French rationalists of the eighteenth century and the attacks on religion of the nineteenth century. He came to see the need to mobilize highly educated Christians, equipped to hold positions of power; he would turn the tide against the *Institución Libre de Enseñanza* and its members. In 1932 Herrera set up an academy in Madrid for the study of law. In 1933 he offered Escrivá a job in the spiritual direction of priests. Escrivá declined, and in the same year set up, himself, a residence for university students. Here was the shape of things to come: a group of Catholic lay-people, disciplined and dedicated, living out their faith in their daily professional life; and so, quietly and one by one, attracting those around them back to Catholic faith and life – and salvation. 'Winning new apostles,' Escrivá would write in *The Way*: 'it is the unmistakeable sign of true zeal. Yours is only a small love, if you are not zealous for the salvation of all souls. The harvest indeed is great, but the labourers are few' (793, 796, 800).

Ever since Escrivá's arrival in Madrid, his confessor had been a Jesuit. This priest had every reason to know how Escrivá's plans were evolving, and one day asked him, 'So how is this work of God going?' The name stuck: *Opus Dei*, the Work of God.

Escrivá's Spain: A Gathering Storm

Josemaría Escrivá found clarity just as his country was falling into the darkest, most turbulent confusion. In April 1931 the King was deposed and a Republic was declared. The new government was determined to separate Church and State and to reduce the Church's influence over education. Legislation came thick and fast: compulsory religious education was ended; the choice of religion was made free. A new Constitution in December drove the programme further: financial support from the government to the Church was ended; religious orders were prohibited from being involved in education, industry or commerce; any order that 'imposed a vow of obedience to an authority distinct from the State' was disbanded and its property seized. This was a straightforward attack on the Jesuits; they were dissolved in 1932 and their schools were closed. 'Spain', declared Azaña, the new Prime Minister, 'is no longer Catholic.'

The Church did all it could to resist. Cardinal Segura urged the National Confederation of Catholic Syndicates in 1928 to serve faithfully 'our august king who cares especially for the Catholic worker'. The largest such syndicate, *Acción Católica*, declared its congress in 1929 to be 'the first mobilization of the Catholic forces of Spain'. And how large were those forces? In many agricultural areas they were overwhelming. But in one working-class parish of Madrid – to take just one urban example – the Church had little more than a fingerhold: only 7 per cent of the parishioners attended Mass; only 25 per cent of children were baptized; and just 10 per cent of the dying received the last rites.

In 1936 the clouds of civil war, which had loured for so long over Spain, at last let loose a torrential storm. The first victim was the Church. In an initial flood of fury and hatred – and then in a chilling campaign that lasted for months – over 8,000 priests, monks and nuns were killed. Lay Catholics were killed too: in some cases simply for membership of a religious association or for wearing a religious medal or other

27

symbol of belief. In Barcelona the cloistered convents were invaded, the nuns 'set free' and their possessions exposed to view: among them were the instruments of self-mortification, misinterpreted by the anti-clerical press as instruments of sexual perversion or of torture.

Madrid was initially in the hands of the anti-clerical Left, the Republicans. Escrivá, like other priests, had to hide for months; eventually he found refuge in the Honduran consulate. He and a group of followers finally escaped to Burgos, the capital of the right-wing Nationalists commanded by the *Caudillo*, the Leader – General Franco. Escrivá would be back: in 1939 he accompanied Franco's troops on the very day they finally captured Madrid after two years of siege, and established Franco's control of the country. The military start to Franco's 'crusade' was won.

That November, a state-funded research institute was founded with effective control over large parts of Spain's education. Its first director was a member of Opus; he stayed in post until 1966, and was followed by a second member. The institute's publication *Arbor* was dominated by members; it has been estimated that between 1939 and 1951 25 per cent of all posts in state universities went to members of Opus, well known to be such and nicknamed '*Opusdeistas*'. But the members of Opus did not stop there; they would soon be playing larger and more visible roles in the public life of Spain.

5

Opus Dei: The Secret Service
of the Catholic Church?

In the fierce heat of that Spanish crucible, Opus Dei
took shape. Let's watch Josemaría Escrivá draw from
the fire the elements he needed and hammer them into
the organization that still exists today. Opus offered –
and still offers – to lay-people and secular priests, the
discipline and rigour and community that had tradi-
tionally been offered to members of religious orders.

In 1950 Opus was given definitive approval by
the Vatican to be a secular institute. We find in its
Constitutions of 1950 just what we would expect
from the Spain of its time. Opus Dei was to achieve,
among the highly educated, what the Jesuits too
had tried to achieve among their pupils. But all the
dangers – or perhaps even the mistakes – of the Jesuits
were to be avoided. Opus was not a 'religious' order;
it included both clergy and lay-people, men and
women. (It did not include members of religious
orders, such as monks – nor does it today. Dan
Brown's Silas could not possibly be a member of
Opus!) Opus acted in humility; it made no claims for
itself, sought no attention or status. It was to run no

newspaper, nor take any part or party-line in the social or political questions of the day.

According to the Constitutions, Opus Dei 'is to work with all its strength so that the so-called intellectual class – which, on account of its learning, its posts or its prestige is a guide for civil society – might adhere to the precepts of Christ' (5). Its members will make a special effort in the spiritual and professional formation of youth, and especially of university students (18 P 3). Public office, especially in roles of leadership, gives members a good opportunity for their apostolic work (201–4). Members ought to be among the more select members of their own class and exercise their apostolate through friendship and trust (186). So Opus Dei 'operates through its members, who expand themselves like rays from a centre, each reaching to his own sphere of action'.

'In order to reach its goals more effectively, Opus Dei wishes to live as hidden; so it refrains from collective actions and has no name . . . by which members are known.' Its members should not engage collectively in public displays of worship (189). The lay members never wear a distinctive sign of their membership (5, 6). 'The number of members is kept hidden from outsiders.' Discretion is vital. 'Lack of this discretion can constitute a grave obstacle to exercising apostolic work or create some difficulty in the context of one's natural family or in the exercise of one's profession.' Thus members 'are to keep a prudent silence regarding the names of other members; and are never to reveal that they themselves are members of Opus Dei . . . without express permission from their local director' (191). This secrecy had already been causing concern among the Spanish bishops in the early 1940s; hardest to discern were the society's Co-operators, people who supported Opus informally.

Escrivá insisted on the society's utter loyalty to the Pope, to the Catholic Church and to Catholic doctrine. He fends off any suggestion that his institute might generate a rival hierarchy within a diocese (82 S 1). The danger was clear: an institute of priests and lay-people, men and women, under regional control – this could all too easily come to resemble a sect, a self-contained church within the Church.

And was Opus Dei a Right-wing political power? Is it still? In Spain in the 1950s and 1960s, members of Opus came to wield enormous power. General Franco was surrounded by groups battling for positions of influence. In 1957 the far-right Falangists, violent and increasingly anti-clerical, seemed likely to dominate the cabinet. The Catholic hierarchy was appalled, and urged Franco to appoint men more sympathetic to the Church; the Ministries of Commerce and Finance and Economic Planning were given to members of Opus. They collaborated on a plan for the economic transformation of the country into a modern, capitalist economy that could take its place in what is now the European Economic Community. As the cabinet members of Opus planned for the post-Franco future, so did Escrivá himself. He wrote about it to Pope Paul VI as early as 1964. He warned that if a revolution were to break out, stopping it would be very difficult. The whole

Church – not just Opus – would be made scapegoats. An evolution in the regime must be set in train, to avoid the threat of anarchy and communism. The solution did not lie in a single Catholic party in Spain, 'because it could begin by being useful to the Church and end up by using her'.

The technocrats of Opus Dei were not above suspicion. In 1969 a corruption scandal broke: a company run by a member of Opus had apparently misappropriated a huge sum of state funds and channelled it to other companies run by members. Three ministers and the Governor of the Bank of Spain – all members of Opus – were implicated; two were quickly reshuffled out of office. The opponents of Opus saw their chance to trump their adversaries, but they overplayed their hand. They talked up the crisis. Such a scandal did not suit Franco at all; he sided *with* Opus. In a new cabinet, the technocratic members of Opus controlled the ministries of Education, Information and Foreign Affairs, Finance, Commerce, Industry and the Development Plan; a further member was Secretary-General of the Francoist 'Moviemento' itself. The former Minister of Information, displaced by one of these *Opusdeistas*, believed that 'the diversity of their opinions and conduct obeyed a co-ordinated plan and that various persons were moving to opportune spaces on the political and economic playing-board'. It is said that Franco, faced with such complaints, brought one conversation to an abrupt end: 'What have you got against the Opus? Because while they work you just f*** about.'

The government sought administrative and economic, but not political, liberalization; as protests grew from the Left and from Basque nationalists – supported with increasing boldness by the Catholic hierarchy – the government was divided between the technocrats of Opus and those on the ultra-Right who called for (and secured) a ferocious judicial clampdown. Right-wing demonstrations were staged, complete with banners: '*Franco si, Opus no! – Franco yes, Opus no!*' At a demonstration arranged by the ultra-Right, anti-Opus slogans were chanted and Opus' 'white freemasonry' was condemned. In January 1974 the ultra-Right won back the government for themselves; the overt dominance of Opus Dei was at an end.

But Opus' reputation was made.

It was a reputation for the persistent, covert, conspiratorial search for power. And what is supposed to be the target now, for Opus' machinations? The Vatican. We have seen that the insights and ideals of Opus Dei were forged in the frightening years in Spain before World War Two. I suspect that the current theories of an Opus Dei conspiracy are in fact an echo, still sounding, of Spanish politics *after* the war.

And beyond the Vatican? Is Opus Dei, in the English-speaking world, secretly weaving a Right-wing web through the Catholic Church, through politics and through business life? Let's end this chapter with a glance at the suspicions to which Opus gives rise today. I should make clear that I am not a Roman Catholic. But I am the first to acknowledge that Escrivá drew up a programme for a determined, focused and highly effective organization that takes seriously the call to prayer, self-restraint and hard work. Escrivá insisted that Opus Dei was a family, its members bound to each other with all the bonds of love and care that unite a family. But, he said, 'our institute is also an army. It is a family without the inconvenience of carnal affection; an army most suited to the struggle by the force of its more severe discipline' (Constitutions 197). No wonder it fosters enormous drive and energy within and among its members. The question in the air is this: what exactly, in the medium and long term, are these members trying to achieve with that energy, and how?

Opus seeks to win and save souls. Escrivá knew of the lament that the environment is such a strong influence on present-day Catholics. He responded fiercely that members must discover what Jesus' first followers discovered: 'How great is our influence on our environment!' (Escrivá, *The Way*, 376). Escrivá wrote of holy intransigence and holy coercion (387). First, for intransigence: 'A man ready to compromise would condemn Jesus to death again . . . To compromise is a sure sign of not possessing the truth' (393–4). Then, for coercion: when it comes to 'saving the Life of so many who are bent on killing their souls', coercion becomes 'holy coercion' (399). It has been claimed that Opus Dei's members, when they target a possible recruit, hide their true intentions behind a façade of friendship; for they are really motivated, at all times, by Escrivá's command, 'Compel them to come in!' We should hardly be surprised. Escrivá was simply quoting a story told by Jesus: a householder who has prepared a banquet finds his invitations rebuffed, so sends his servants out 'into the highways and byways' with the command: 'Compel them to come in, so that my house may be full!' (Luke 14.23).

Times change. The society's discretion had been invaluable in the Spain of the 1930s; in the England of the 1970s it looked furtive and deceitful. 'Holy coercion' had been fitting in a Spain whose Church still thought of every Spaniard as her child; in England of the 1970s it looked like bullying and spiritual blackmail. The member of a religious order owes total and ungrudging obedience to his or her superior; most adults in modern British or American society acknowledge no such duty to anyone. The nurture, outside the religious orders, of the loyalties and bonds associated with such orders was thrilling in a country in which religious orders had for centuries played a leading role in national life; in liberal, Protestant England it seemed to be the sign of a cult.

In the late 1970s complaints about Opus Dei reached Basil Hume, the Roman Catholic Archbishop of Westminster. New statutes were being drawn up for Opus, but were not yet in place. Basil Hume saw the draft statutes, and as a temporary measure in December 1981 published – for anyone to read – a set of guidelines. Every word of these guidelines betrays a real concern that moral and spiritual power (especially over young people) was being secretly sought and improperly used. The guidelines brought Opus out of the shadows and into a glare of accusations and suspicion. Here is an extract:

– It is essential that young people who wish to join Opus Dei should first discuss the matter with their parents or legal guardians. If there are, by exception, good reasons for not approaching their families, these reasons should, in every case, be discussed with the local bishop or his delegate.

– While it is accepted that those who join Opus Dei take on the proper duties and responsibilities of membership, care must be taken to respect the freedom of the individual; first, the freedom of the individual to join or to leave the organization without undue pressure being exerted; secondly, the freedom of the individual at any stage to choose his or her own spiritual director, whether or not the director is a member of Opus Dei.

– Initiatives and activities of Opus Dei, within the diocese of Westminster, should carry a clear indication of their sponsorship and management.

In 1982 the status of Opus Dei changed; the new statutes were finalized. These are based on the 1950 Constitutions; but the emphases have shifted. There is far less attention paid to the priesthood. The rules on discretion are completely redrawn; gone is the demand for 'prudent silence' about other members.

So Opus Dei has moved on. But nothing like as fast as the world in which it lives. Opus Dei is still giving its 'army', marshalled against the liberalism of today, the same training and discipline it provided against the Spanish radicalism of 1936. Is this a weakness? By Opus' own lights, certainly not. It is Opus' greatest

'Fact' – or Fiction?

Silas and that Cilice

We hear several times in *The Da Vinci Code* about the – agonizing – studded belt (cilice) that Silas wears on his thigh. In Opus' 1982 statutes it is worth reading the full paragraph on such practices. Members of religious orders may well subdue the flesh by corporal mortification; but for many of us – as for that mob in Spain, all those years ago – the idea is alien, even kinky. The statutes give a full, clear account of the reasons for undergoing such mortification. We should not be put off by the register in which this rule is written; it is worth tuning in to this style of language we do not often hear:

> In order to conquer the snares of concupiscence – especially the pride of life, which could feed on theory, social status, and professional work – Christian ascetical demands are to be firmly and deeply cultivated by the faithful of the Prelature. This asceticism rests upon the faithful and perpetual sense of humility, individual and collective; on the brilliance of connatural simplicity; on the familiar and noble plan of activity; on constant expression of serenely flowing joy; on work, self-denial, sobriety, acts of sacrifice and on performing established exercises of corporal mortification every day and week, according to each one's age and condition. They cultivate all of these, as a means not only of personal purification, but also of true and solid spiritual progress, in keeping with

those tried and true words 'You will only accomplish as much as you bring about by force against yourself.' They are also cared for as the necessary preparation to accomplish any apostolate in society and to perfect its exercise: 'I complete,' wrote St Paul, 'what is lacking in the passion of Christ in my flesh for his body, which is the Church' (Colossians 1.24).

Statutes 1982, 83 S 1

strength. The dangers to the faithful are not, of course, so immediate or physical as they were in the years before the Spanish Civil War; but the danger to the faith is undiminished. A great deal about Opus Dei is unfashionable; but it is true to itself, and true to the command given in Jesus' story by the host who has prepared his great feast: 'Compel them to come in' (Luke 14.23).

So there we have it: almost 80 years of Opus Dei. If you admired Opus Dei when you started reading these two chapters, you will probably admire it still – and perhaps more heartily than ever. And if you distrusted it then, you will probably distrust it still.

In *The Da Vinci Code*, Dan Brown sets up Opus as the enemy of that sexual fulfilment represented (according to his characters) by Jesus and Mary Magdalene. We can see why. The central power in Opus is in the hands of male, celibate priests. Individual houses are run by celibates. Women in

Opus Dei: Some Facts and Figures

How many people are involved in Opus Dei today? According to the Vatican, Opus Dei in 2004 had 85,491 members; of these 1,850 are priests. There are about 164,000 Co-operators – active friends of the organization – and another 900,000 people around the world who attend Opus Dei meetings. These form a tiny proportion of the Catholic Church worldwide. Do they punch above their weight? Yes, almost certainly; that, after all, was Escrivá's own hope for Opus' highly educated members in their positions of influence.

How wealthy is Opus Dei? I can only draw on the latest estimate: that in the USA at the end of 2002, foundations and other institutions affiliated to Opus Dei controlled $344 million. The sums themselves tell only part of the story; a well-organized, disciplined and focused group of people with shared ideals and aims can achieve far more, with the same resources, than a flaccid or divided organization. ('We do not spend our time building buildings,' declare the 1950 Constitutions, 227; 'rather, we take for our own buildings already constructed.' This has certainly changed; in the 1990s, Opus Dei used most of a bequest of some $78 million to build a 17-storey headquarters in Manhattan.)

Spain, 70 years ago, were expected to keep house for the family; in Opus Dei's centres, the celibate assistants who keep house are all women. Opus no longer emphasizes a hierarchy within Opus itself in the power and standing of priests, of other celibate men, of celibate women in various roles and of married people. But even a neutral observer may think Opus does not need to – it *embodies* such a hierarchy in its structure.

What of those other concerns to which Opus has given rise? Does Opus seek to attract and mould members by re-socializing them, by fostering close 'family' bonds of affection and loyalty within the society? Yes. Does it call for sustained physical, mental and spiritual self-restraint and discipline? Yes. These are characteristics of formal religious orders throughout Christian history. For Opus Dei, which is not an order, Escrivá adopted precisely the characteristics of such orders that, he believed, would nurture his own members.

Have these demands made some members, who are out of place in such a community, desperately unhappy? Yes. Has the society's response made things worse rather than better? In some cases, almost certainly. These are dangers in religious orders too, unless the superiors are of outstanding generosity and wisdom.

Opus Dei will continue to stir intense loyalty and intense suspicion. Loyalty comes from those Roman Catholics who insist that individual Catholics should regain the vigour and rigour of an obedient faith, in disciplined resistance to the thoughtless self-indulgence of the twenty-first century. Suspicion comes from those who believe such Catholics are blind to the unsettling truths about human nature, society and power that the rationalists and heirs of the

Enlightenment – and, as some Catholics would insist, the grace of God himself – have revealed to us.

This disagreement has already been dividing the Roman Catholic Church itself for 100 years. It is genuine, deep and important. I *suspect* that Opus Dei, so conspicuously loyal to the conservative Roman Catholic hierarchy, is in part a punch-bag for resentment or distrust of this hierarchy itself. Opus will be taking a lot more blows, in the years to come.

For almost the whole of *The Da Vinci Code*, Silas is a frightening fanatic and Bishop Aringarosa is a sinister schemer. But at the end, everything changes. The last scenes featuring Silas and the Bishop are among the best, most touching passages in the book. Silas shoots his beloved patron by mistake, realizes that he has been utterly duped by the Teacher, and dies at last as he had so nearly died when Aringarosa rescued him all those years before. And the Bishop? We have thought him the villain of the piece. But he too has been duped. Dan Brown, as ever enjoying a pun, has allowed himself a smile at our expense. 'Aringarosa' is – as nearly as may be – the Italian for 'red herring'. That is exactly what the Bishop has been in all the convolutions of the plot: a hugely compelling *aringa rosa*.

Part 3
Leonardo: *The Last Supper*

6

Decoding the Code:
Is Mary Magdalene in
The Last Supper?

It is time to go back through the centuries: to 1494, in
the north Italian city of Milan, where Leonardo da
Vinci was starting work on his masterpiece, *The Last
Supper*. He had been commissioned to decorate the
wall of a monastic dining-hall in Milan. It took him
five years. It quickly became known as one of the
great paintings in Europe. Within 50 years, however,
it was known too as a technical disaster. Leonardo's
masterpiece was falling apart.

In our generation (until *The Da Vinci Code* was
published!) Leonardo's *Last Supper* was chiefly
famous for being a ruin. But this is not what made it
so triumphantly famous when it was first finished.
Let's see why it was recognized, from the moment
Leonardo put down his brushes, as one of the greatest
paintings in Europe. And then we will be able to
answer the question raised by Dan Brown: Who is the
figure seated to the right of Jesus in the painting? Is it
Mary Magdalene?

The Last Supper: Damp and Disaster

Over the course of three centuries, Italian artists had mastered the technique of painting successfully on walls. By the 1430s the procedure was uniform. Each morning wet plaster was applied to an area of the wall that the artist could paint on that day, while the plaster was still wet. The painter used a water-soluble paint, which soaked into the plaster. As the plaster dried, the paint dried in it, as part of it. And for as long as the plaster survives – in many cases, right through to the present day – the paint survives too.

This is an effective technique. But the artist must work fast; Leonardo always worked slowly, with painstaking care. And the wall in Milan was clearly affected by damp, from which the painting would need protection. So Leonardo, for his *Last Supper*, abandoned water-based paint and wet plaster. He applied to the wall a compound of his own devising: a mix of plaster, pitch and mastic. He let it dry to the consistency of stone. To this he applied his paint, an emulsion to stick to the surface of the compound. The results were spectacular; but they did not last. As anyone knows who has applied emulsion to a damp wall, the damp will sooner or later work its way to the surface; the paint will blister, crack and come loose. The triumph of Leonardo's *Last Supper* became a tragedy.

The painting is a wreck, but its composition is clear. And this is enough to reveal why the painting became so famous so quickly. Leonardo painted a Last Supper unlike any other. Around Jesus, in all the disciples, is raw passion: shock, fear, anger – and guilt. *Guilt*: for there is a traitor in their midst.

What did any viewer expect to see, who was about to encounter a painting of the Last Supper? Jesus, at the centre of the painting and, around him, his twelve closest friends and followers, his disciples. The atmosphere should be stately and still. A sacred ritual is being enacted. Jesus often has in front of him a large cup, and a platter of bread. He is about to utter the words still familiar, even today, at every celebration of the Mass or Holy Communion. Jesus faces the viewer. For the words he said then to his disciples are, for Christians, the words (slightly adapted) he still addresses today, through the minister or priest, to his followers. First, over the bread:

'Take and eat from this, all of you; for this is my body.'

And then, over the cup:

'Take and drink from it, all of you; for this is the cup of my blood, of the new and eternal covenant, the mystery of faith, which will be shed for you and for many for forgiveness of sins. As often as you do this, you will do it for my remembrance.'

On the right-hand side of Jesus, his 'Beloved Disciple' should recline on his breast. John's Gospel speaks of this disciple at various crucial moments in the story of Jesus; but never gives his name. According to ancient tradition, this disciple was John himself. He lived for 60 years after Jesus' death; and, as an old man, he wrote the Gospel that bears his name. No wonder he is always shown, next to Jesus, as a young and beardless man.

One other figure matters: the traitor, Judas Iscariot. Most artists showed him way out to one side. Sometimes he was even shown across the table, separated from Jesus and all the other – loyal – disciples. Judas was the treasurer of Jesus' entourage, and (John tells us in his Gospel) an embezzler; Judas almost always clasps a money-bag.

Any monks in Milan who processed into their dining-hall in 1499 to see Leonardo's painting for the first time knew what to expect. They were in for a surprise.

Let's look more closely at the painting; the illustration on the front cover of this book is large enough to show us the details we need to see. At the centre, in the background, is an open doorway flanked by narrower windows. Through the openings we see a north Italian landscape; it is still light outside. These openings invite us to think of the painting as a 'triptych', a painting in three panels; this was one of the most famous and familiar forms that an altarpiece could take in Leonardo's day. In a triptych, the central and wider panel is occupied by the most important figure or figures of the painting: generally Jesus, often shown, for example, as an infant with his mother

Mary. Leonardo's Jesus is duly framed by the door-way behind him. No other figure breaks into that opening. Jesus has the calm dignity that was expected in the central figure of a triptych.

Each of the two side-panels of a triptych was, in general, half the width of the central panel; they were often hinged to its frame, so that they could be closed over it. In these side-panels were painted subsidiary figures, often saints, looking inwards to the central figure in adoration. Here Leonardo has wrought havoc with his viewers' expectations. His subsidiary figures are almost everywhere they should not be. On Jesus' left, two figures crowd into the side-panel; a third, standing, leans towards it. On Jesus' right – in the painting's most important and poignant detail – his neighbour leans as far as possible away from him. Who is this neighbour? The Beloved Disciple, the one person above all others whom Jesus needs to have near him.

Where, then, is the cup that should be in front of Jesus? It is not there. There is just a jug of water near Jesus, and several glasses of wine along the length of the table. And the bread? There are just small loaves, scattered over the table. *Leonardo has not depicted the standard moment in the Last Supper at all.*

We need to run through the story again. Jesus and his disciples had gathered on that solemn evening before his arrest, trial and crucifixion. What else happened, that we have not heard of yet? We read in John's Gospel:

Jesus was troubled in spirit and testified, 'Truly, truly, I say to you, one of you will betray me.' The disciples looked at one another, not knowing who he was talking about.

One of his disciples was reclining on the breast of Jesus; it was the one that Jesus loved. So Simon Peter nodded to him, and said to him, 'Who is it, that he is talking about?'

(John 13.21–24, Latin version)

This is the scene shown by Leonardo.

Jesus has just spoken of the traitor. On Jesus' left, three disciples form a group. They are appalled. James leans back in horror, arms outstretched. Thomas raises one finger to get Jesus' attention. Philip has stood up; he leans forwards, his hands on his chest as if to say, 'Lord, it is not me, you know it is not me.' James and Thomas fill – and more than fill – the space of the side-panel behind them. Philip leans towards it.

And on Jesus' right? Here, beside Jesus, is a gap.

The Beloved Disciple is indeed on Jesus' right. But he is not reclining on Jesus' breast. He is leaning far to his own right, his face turned away from Jesus. Simon Peter, two places further along the table, has beckoned to him and now leans towards him, behind and past the disciple in between. Peter has one hand on the shoulder of the Beloved Disciple. He is asking, 'Find out who is the traitor.'

In his other hand, hidden from the view of Jesus, Peter is holding a knife. This is the Peter who will, in a few hours' time, draw a sword against Jesus' enemies and wound one of them before Jesus stops the fighting. Peter already has violence in mind – against the traitor, here and now. But he needs to know, Who is it? Who is the traitor?

In between Peter and the Beloved Disciple sits a bearded figure. Of all the faces in the painting, only his face is in shade. His left hand is reaching towards a loaf of bread. In his right hand is a money-bag. This is Judas. The man who will betray Jesus. He is sitting right at the centre of the group, can overhear Peter and the Beloved Disciple, and is within inches of Peter's knife. The man whom Simon and the Beloved Disciple are trying to identify is sitting in between them.

Peter is thinking of violence. Jesus is not. He is going to his death, and he knows it. He will not resist. How little even his closest friends and pupils understand. At the very moment when Jesus is in the greatest need of their support, his dearest friend is leaning as far away from him as possible – both physically and emotionally. He is being drawn into a plan to do murder. Between Jesus and the Beloved Disciple there is a gap far wider than just the wall behind them.

No painting of the Last Supper could be more poignant than this. And in this great drama, Mary Magdalene plays no part. Has she then no role at all in the last, climatic scenes of Jesus' life on earth? On the contrary. We shall find in Mary Magdalene the key that unlocks the story of Easter and sets free its many meanings. Robert and Teabing want to do justice to Mary Magdalene. But they cannot, for they have not seen even half of what she has to offer us.

A Man with a Woman's Breasts?

We still need to observe one final detail. Doesn't the figure on the right of Jesus have woman's breasts? Has Leonardo left a clue in his painting that we are still refusing to see – a clue revealing Mary Magdalene at the heart of his composition? No. The folds of this figure's shirt are drawn together by its clasp, just beneath the throat. This clasp gathers the material in folds from left and right across the figure's torso. The figure's arms are lowered, leaving the folds at the height of a woman's breasts. *And three other figures in the painting, whose chests we can see, are wearing the same sort of shirt.*

Might the other three figures with such shirts be women too? No. One is Jesus; the others are heavily bearded disciples. One of them, the third in from the left as we face the painting, has his hands raised, but arms lowered; and his shirt falls across his torso in just the same way as the Beloved Disciple's. These other figures are not women; nor is the figure sitting on the right-hand side of Jesus.

Part 4
The Knights Templar

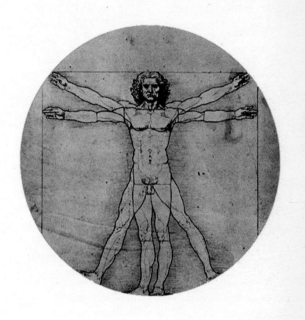

7

The Secrets of Power: Enter the Knights Templar

And so back through the centuries we go: to the Knights Templar. Did the Templars discover proof in Jerusalem that Jesus and Mary Magdalene had been married? Was *this* the source of all their power over kings and popes? Did they guard the grail? Not the holy cup, the *San Greal*, of legend, but the real blood, the *Sang real*, of Jesus – the bloodline of his descendants? This, says Teabing, is the *real* history of the Templars.

Assume, for a moment, that the Templars had known that Jesus was not God but just a married man; that they had even, perhaps, secured a relic of Jesus himself or of Mary Magdalene. The knights might well have treasured the relic; but they would certainly not have worshipped Jesus. As we hear in the novel, stories abounded of the Templars' strange rituals: they denied Christ; they worshipped the statue of a head. To any orthodox Christian, this was blasphemy. The Templars had gone too far. Philip, King of France, had the excuse he needed to rid himself and Europe of this virus. Charges were prepared, and on a single day, Friday 13 October 1307, his agents swooped on every Templar house in France. Even today, all these centuries later, 'Friday the Thirteenth' is a day of ill-omen. The Templars' guilt was assumed. The King had outmanoeuvred them: any knight who appealed to the Templars' great secret about the married Jesus would confirm his blasphemy and expose himself to a terrible death. Defiance was worse than useless. The Templars were at an end.

This is a gripping story. Is it true?

The Templars were founded in the Holy Land in 1120 as a religious order of 'brothers' who took the vows of poverty, chastity and obedience – and who accepted, as well, the particular charge to 'maintain, as far as they could, the roads and highways against the ambushes of thieves and attackers, especially in regard to the safety of pilgrims'. The destination of every pilgrim to the Holy Land was Jerusalem, the centre of the world. The most sacred place within Jerusalem – and so, the centre of the centre of the world – was the Church of the Holy Sepulchre, supposedly the site of Christ's own death, burial and rising. The Church of the Holy Sepulchre is round: giant columns ring its central space and support its upper drum. Between the columns and the outer walls is a walkway for pilgrims.

Thousands upon thousands of such pilgrims, over the centuries, made their pilgrimage to Jerusalem and to the Holy Sepulchre. But could the holiness of the Sepulchre be shared, be somehow made available to those who could never visit it? Yes. By building a replica: a round church, in lands far from Jerusalem, built to recreate the sanctity of the Holy Sepulchre itself.

Sophie, Robert and Teabing come to the Temple Church in London. (This is the Church in which I myself serve as 'Master' and from which I am writing this book.) Its eastern half is a normal church, with aisles and altar. Its western end is round; giant columns ring its central space and support the upper drum. The Round Church was built in the shape of the Holy Sepulchre, and shared its holiness too. For us, the two churches are separated by hundreds of miles. In the imagination of the Templars and of medieval pilgrims, they were not separate at all. Sophie, Robert and Teabing have found Jerusalem in the heart of London.

They have come to the Temple Church in search of an effigy. And here they find a famous set of tombs, carved in stone: the effigies of nine knights; and the plain gravestone of a tenth. Such burial in the Round Church was devoutly to be desired; for burial in the Round was imagined as burial 'in' the Holy Sepulchre, the place of Jesus' own death and burial in Jerusalem.

These cold effigies of the knights in full armour seem fitting memorials to soldiers long dead. But these knights' eyes are open. They are all portrayed as being in their early thirties; this is the age at which Christ died and at which, the Church believed, he would finally raise the dead to life. One knight is shown drawing his sword. Three are shown with crossed legs; in medieval manuscripts and glass, this posture indicates a figure who is walking towards the viewer. According to the Bible, Christ will at the end of the earth's present history return to Jerusalem and summon all of the dead to judgement. And that is where the knights in the Round Church are buried: 'in' Jerusalem. The effigies are not memorials of what has long since been and gone; they speak of what is yet to come, of these once and future knights who are poised to hear Christ's summons, to spring again to life and once more to serve their Lord.

It is a fitting place to wait. For the place of Jesus' death and burial is the place where, according to the New Testament, the risen Jesus was first seen too. Our knights were buried in this re-creation of the garden where Jesus, risen and alive, walked at dawn on Easter Day. They have shared his burial, in the hope and faith that they will share his resurrection.

We cannot possibly do justice to the Templars in a few pages. Let's follow just three threads through their story: their role in the story of the grail; the source of their wealth and power within Europe; and their suppression. Do Dan Brown's characters open our eyes to truths that generations of historians, stuck in the deep old ruts of traditional scholarship, have been unable to see?

8

The Power of Secrets:
The Blood of Jesus, the Templars
and the Holy Grail

In one of the great fictional narratives of the Middle Ages, *Parzival* by Wolfram von Eschenbach, the Templars' great duty was the protection of the grail. The narrative is richly symbolic. Once we look behind its surface-meaning we can find ever more enthralling layers of significance. Perhaps the standard histories of the Templars – telling of pilgrims, politics and war – simply *miss the point*. Does guarding the grail really represent the Templars' most secret and most important calling, to protect the descendants of Jesus, his 'true blood' born from Mary Magdalene? It is a spine-tingling thought. After the next few pages, however, you may reckon that Dan Brown understands the grail narratives from the Middle Ages better than his own characters do. Medieval grail stories involve labyrinthine plots, false leads and the discovery of love. The search for the grail – and the effect of that search on the heroes' character, understanding and human sympathy – is indispensable to and quite as important as the stories' actual denouement. Does this remind you, as it reminds me, of *The Da Vinci Code* itself?

We first hear of the grail in the *Conte du Graal* (*Story of the Grail*), composed by Chrétien of Troyes, a town in Champagne in northern France, in the 1180s. He makes no mention of the Templars at all. And the grail itself? When Chrétien wrote, *graal* was simply a word for a dish used in dining; sometimes it refers to a shallow dish in which morsels of meat, in their own juices, could be handed round. Chrétien's *graal* is apparently such a dish, but invested with strange power. The hero Perceval is told about the *graal* and the king who is served from it: 'Do not imagine that it holds [fish such as] pike, lamprey or salmon. With a single host [*oiste*, as offered and eaten at the Mass or Eucharist], carried to him in the grail, the king nourishes and sustains his life.' Here, then, was a flat dish that could have held a large fish; but instead it had on it just one Eucharistic host. (Chrétien is probably indebted to pagan stories of a magic dish, providing unlimited food.)

Chrétien dedicated his *Conte du Graal* to Philip of Alsace, Count of Flanders, who had been in the Holy Land in 1177 and went back on crusade in September 1190. On that first visit Philip had gone to the grave of his mother, who had died in the Holy Land. There had been hopes that Philip would take over as regent of the Latin Kingdom of Jerusalem from his first-cousin King Baldwin, who was suffering from leprosy; but the hopes came to nothing. How striking it is that Chrétien's hero Perceval sets out to find his mother, who had – unbeknown to him – already died; and that he is first-cousin of the Grail Castle's wounded king. As Philip was preparing to set out once more for Jerusalem, Chrétien was writing of Perceval, whose first visit to the grail had been a failure and who must set out a second time, this time to do his duty. Chrétien's patron was thinking of Jerusalem; Chrétien's readers would think of Jerusalem too.

From Chrétien to his most famous successor; from northern France south-east to Thuringia in the heart of Germany. Here Wolfram von Eschenbach composed his *Parzeval* over several years around 1200. On every page Wolfram's imagination enlarges and enhances Chrétien's tale. Now the grail is guarded in a Temple and its guardians are *Templeisen* – not the usual name for Templars (*Tempelherren*) but clearly intended to evoke the order. And the grail itself? In Wolfram's account, it is not primarily a vessel at all; it is a precious stone, decorated with gold. It still, none the less, has a function at meals: 'Whatever one stretched out one's hand for in the presence of the grail, it was found all ready and to hand: dishes warm, dishes cold, new-fangled dishes and old favourites . . . The grail was a cornucopia of the sweets of this world; it scarcely fell short of what they tell us of the heavenly Kingdom.'

Parzeval learns more from a hermit, on Good Friday, the day of Jesus' crucifixion. The *Templeisen*, says the hermit, 'live from a stone of purest kind. It is called *lapsit exillis*. [It is not clear what Wolfram said here in the performance of his poem; medieval scribes were already baffled.] . . . Further: however ill a mortal may be, from the day on which he sees the stone he cannot die for that week . . . This stone is also called the grail . . . Today is Good Friday, when one can always see a dove wing its way down from heaven. It brings a small white wafer [once more, the Eucharistic host] to the stone and leaves it there.' From this wafer 'the stone receives all that is good on earth of food and drink'. So here is Wolfram's grail: it is guarded by *Templeisen*; but it is not a cup and it holds no blood.

Why did Wolfram introduce the 'Templars'? He had picked up the clues left by Chrétien, pointing to the Holy Land, and he had good reasons of his own to want his Grail Castle to be imagined as Jerusalem: his own patron, Hermann I, Landgrave of Thuringia, went on the German crusade, 1197–98. But Wolfram himself had no links with Chrétien's Philip of Alsace or his journeys to the Holy Land; and by the time Wolfram was telling the story the crusaders' dynastic complexities – in both Europe and the Middle East – had changed. Chrétien's clues were no longer easy to follow; Wolfram must devise some of his own.

And he does. Wolfram's Grail Castle, *Munsalvaesche*, stands on a hill as Jerusalem stands on Mount Sion. *Munsalvaesche* may be read as meaning Mount Savage; but Wolfram's own poetic heirs understood it as Mount of Salvation – vividly recalling the holy mountain of Jerusalem. Wolfram appropriately introduces, as the guardians of *Munsalvaesche*, the *Templeisen* – and with their name evokes the

Templars, first and most famous of all the orders that protected Jerusalem.

Wolfram's account was gripping; but it had competition. In the same years the story was being brilliantly re-worked by Robert de Boron in his *Joseph of Arimathea*. Robert gave to the story of the grail the shape it has had ever since. He tells of the 'very noble vessel' in which 'Christ performed his sacrament' at the Last Supper. This vessel reached Pontius Pilate, and when Jesus' disciple Joseph of Arimathea came to Pilate to ask permission to take down the body of Jesus from the cross and to bury it, Pilate gave him the vessel. Joseph released and lowered Jesus' body, and found that it was still bleeding; Joseph caught the blood in that same vessel. And how are we to envisage it?

Robert no doubt knew of one poignant tradition (familiar from the ninth century onwards) in paintings of the crucifixion: a woman, representing the Church, holds a cup in which she catches the blood and water that pour from the wound in Christ's side; so the Church, at every celebration of the Mass, offered up in the chalice the blood and water of Christ. Was the vessel in Robert's poem, then, a cup? Robert took care. He would want to make an explicit link between the Eucharist, the crucifixion *and* Chrétien's grail. The blood of Christ was linked – at the Eucharist and in those paintings of the crucifixion – with a deep, steep-sided cup: a chalice. But Chrétien's grail had been a shallow dish that held a Eucharistic host.

How was Robert to unite them? He has Jesus himself explain to Joseph of Arimathea, in a vision, that the vessel of the Last Supper, 'this vessel in which you put my blood when you collected it from my body, will be called "chalice".' Robert later introduces a character called Petrus, clearly named to evoke Simon Peter. Petrus names this same vessel the grail; for 'whosoever sees the *grail* will find it *agree*able'. Robert has now identified the cup that (as Robert himself said) had held Christ's blood with the grail that (as Chrétien said) held the 'host' of Christ's body.

Robert ends by telling of the grail's journey from the Holy Land to the West. The familiar story of the grail is under way. For Robert's heirs, the Holy Cup, *San Greal*, had held the true blood, *Sang real*, of Jesus. By 1450 the English poet Henry Lovelich, translating from French, is spelling out the ambiguity for his readers. His Merlin tells the king about the supper that Joseph of Arimathea was ordered to arrange after Jesus' death. Joseph had used the grail: 'Sire,' explains Merlin, 'this people called this vessel the *Sank Ryal* or else *Seint Graal*.' The pun exploited by Dan Brown's characters is a pun well known in the Middle Ages; but it evoked the past – the life and death of Jesus himself – not the future of his imagined blood-line.

So there we have it. The grail was an invention by Chrétien; the Templars' involvement was an invention by Wolfram. Wolfram and Robert are both Chrétien's heirs; each develops the story in his own way. In Wolfram's account we have *Templeisen* but no cup. In Robert's, we have a cup but no Templars;

and the Templars will play no explicit part in any other thirteenth-century romance of the grail.

Has *The Da Vinci Code* nothing, then, to tell us about the grail? On the contrary. Anyone who has enjoyed the novel is set fair to enjoy the grail-romances from the Middle Ages. Dan Brown is an heir of Chrétien, Wolfram and Robert.

Let's be clear about Chrétien and Wolfram: they were not composing a geography of the knightly world; they were allowing hints and clues to work their magic. Jerusalem was an earthly city, of course: the destination of earthly pilgrims and protected by earthly knights. But it was as well the symbol of its own heavenly counterpart: the destination of all the faithful after death, when their pilgrimage on earth was ended and due penance for wrongdoings paid. Jerusalem was the symbol too for the faith which had been founded there in the death and rising of Christ: the faith which Christian knights must forever be loyal to, love and defend.

The search for the grail may seem – not least to the heroes who undertake it – a search for a special thing in a special place. But the heroes become worthy of the thing and place only on and through the search itself: as they grow in wisdom, maturity and a heart-felt human sympathy. They lose their families and fail to recognize close relations; they fall in and out of love; they bluster with pride and self-assurance. As the stories unfold they rediscover their families; they find their true and lasting love; they grow in humility. The medieval poets understood the quest better than their heroes; and Dan Brown understands it better than his. For he has written the story of a modern grail and modern quest. Sophie comes to understand and forgive her grandfather, and rediscovers the rest of her family. Robert, so knowing at the novel's start, must gain the true knowledge that comes from loyalty and love. By the time he kneels before the inverse pyramid in the Louvre, on the last page of the novel, he has discovered far more than a pile of bones.

9
The Templars:
A Medieval Multinational

Whatever gave the real Templars their power, it was not the grail. We have to look elsewhere. For a couple of pages we are going to survey their banking operations. I will have to decouple – quite improperly – the order's financial dealings from their religious and military life. But this will at least bring those financial dealings, too often ignored, under the spotlight; and will dissolve some of the mists and mystery that obscure our view of the order's life as a whole.

Nearly 700 years after the Templars vanished from history, we can still catch glimpses of their wealth. The Temple Church itself is a majestic chapel built in the most modern styles of the twelfth and thirteenth centuries. All around me is the area still known as 'The Temple', occupied by the knights from the 1180s and strategically placed mid-way, even then, between the merchants in the City of London and the king's court in Westminster. Dotted round Britain are place-names that still evoke the order: Temple Bruer, Temple Combe, Temple Cowley, Temple Dinsley, Temple Meads.

Far grander than the Temple in London was the Paris Temple: an enormous complex (destroyed in the French Revolution) that served for over 100 years as the treasury of the kings of France. Through the thirteenth century, the standard *livre*, whose weight and purity were normative for every *livre* put into circulation, was kept there. A map of medieval Europe would show at least 870 Templar castles or houses and (according to one critic of the order) 9,000 Templar manors. A library of their charters and deeds would show them managing their endowments with vigour: endlessly extending, rationalizing and improving their lands.

But we have so far heard only one side of this story. We have not mentioned the Templars' outgoings. In the Middle East, castles had to be built or bought, maintained and manned; an army of knights had to be supported in a hostile, arid country hundreds of miles from home; a fleet of ships had to supply them. The Templars' houses in the West were obliged to commit one-third of their income to the support of operations in the East. Special crises or needs called for special exactions: to buy the city of Sidon, for instance, in 1260; or to enlarge the fleet in the 1290s, when all the Eastern fortresses had been lost. At one point the Templars began to buy the whole island of Cyprus, to be their own independent state; but the project was apparently too ambitious, even for them.

It is humbling even to envisage the financial, logistical, building and military skills that the Templars had to master and co-ordinate to keep their forces in the field.

The Templars' Army

How many men did the order have in the Middle East? Estimates vary: between 300 and 600 knights, and up to 2,000 sergeants; each knight was entitled to three horses, each sergeant to one. The costs were high, and rising. In the 1180s a knight in France itself needed the income from 750 acres to equip and maintain himself as a mounted warrior; by the 1260s he would need the income from 3,750 acres. The price of horses doubled between 1140 and 1180, and doubled again by 1220.

If the Templars could manage their own endowments and income so effectively, then they could manage other people's. Templar treasuries in the West were (generally) secure from attack; the Templars were perceived to be honest; they had unrivalled experience in the control of large and complex assets. What they did for themselves, they were soon doing for nobles, kings and popes. This sounds less dramatic than knights mounted on their chargers and ready for battle; but we have learnt afresh, in recent years, that no war can be won without the investment and management of enormous resources. A cash crisis can be as dangerous to a campaign as the most determined enemy.

The Templars: Credit, Cash-flow and the Crusades

Let's hear of the most perilous moments in the 1250s and 1260s: just a few years in the West's long attempt to hold the Latin kingdom of Jerusalem. In 1250, King Louis IX of France and his army were captured in Egypt and must be ransomed. Some 200,000 *livres* ('pounds') were needed straightaway, for the king himself to be released. The army's main funds were at Acre, by now the headquarters of all the military orders, 250 miles to the north; and the king's advisers in Egypt found themselves 30,000 *livres* short. They approached the Templars, who had a ship, moored off the coast, in which they were holding the moneys entrusted to them by the soldiers of Louis' army. The Templars insisted that they could not use the deposits of those other clients to redeem the king; but (to find a solution to the crisis) made it plain that they would put up only a token resistance if the king's agents offered violence – which those agents duly did.

In 1251 some of Louis' ships, carrying money to the crusaders, sank at sea. No wonder he increased his use of bills of exchange to provide cash to the Middle East. He could raise money in the East, chiefly from Italian (most often Genoese) merchants based there. His agents gave them bills to be drawn on the Temple in Paris; so the merchants, via their own agents in Paris, could repatriate their assets without risk of any loss at sea. Despite the Church's prohibition of usury, Louis was (covertly) paying 20 per cent interest.

By 1260 the crusaders in Acre itself were in imminent danger of defeat and were critically short of funds. Credit was hard to come by; most of the Italian banker-merchants had already left the city. The Templars in Acre wrote to their leaders in the West, who sent on urgent letters and messengers, pleading for help, to the Pope, kings and magnates. The crisis did not ease. In 1264, to free up credit, Louis wrote to his agents in the Holy Land: they were to borrow 4,000 *livres* locally in the king's name for the crusaders' use. The loan would be repaid on presentation of the king's letter at the Paris Temple. The agents sought the help of the two most famous military orders, the Knights Templar and Knights Hospitaller. The orders offered to indemnify the lenders against loss and – with the Patriarch of Jerusalem – to issue a signed receipt. Merchants were found, the money was lent, a crisis in cash-flow was averted once more.

The Templars had mastered the complex, roundabout business of international banking. With their military and financial skills together, the knights were vital to the defence of the Holy Land. They became vital too in the domestic economies of successive popes, kings of France and kings of England – not to mention the lesser royalty, nobles and merchants for whom they managed and oversaw transactions without number. (They were not alone. Under King Edward I of England a Knight Hospitaller, the Prior of Clerkenwell, was treasurer of England.)

The Templars' banking gave them vast influence; did it give then an income too? Yes. Late repayment incurred a penalty, sometimes very steep: for a loan of 3,000 *livres* one client agreed to an additional charge, in the event of late repayment, of the same sum again. Clients could make gifts in acknowledgement of the service. And interest was sometimes quite openly levied: in Aragon the Templars charged 10 per cent interest, being 2 per cent less than the maximum allowed to Christian moneylenders and half the rate charged by Jews.

The Templars: No Man Can Serve Two Masters?

The Templars were truly international. By 1214 a Templar was the treasurer to the French king, Philip Augustus. Philip was at war with King John of England, who relied heavily on the Templars. The Templars, then, served both kings at once, on both sides of the war. John gave them two commissions: the Temple in London was to secure the safe arrival in England of some knights from Ponthieu who would fight for John; and the Temple in La Rochelle (whose credit was far better than John's) was to pay a pension to a wavering count to ensure his neutrality in the war. On one occasion the Templars' business acumen landed them in trouble. They fought as bravely as ever in the crusade of Louis IX; but the king was appalled to learn that, during the campaign, the Templars'

Grand Master had (without consulting the king) concluded a land deal with the Sultan of Damascus. Louis forced the Templars to do public penance, and their Master publicly to free the Sultan from the deal.

In the economic machinery of the Middle Ages, the Templars were among the most important cogs of all. Was this because they controlled – and could threaten to reveal – the secret of Jesus' marriage to Mary Magdalene? No. Not at all. A full account of their history would describe – as I conspicuously have not – their commitment and courage in war; in the counsels of the crusaders, nobody could ignore or successfully cross them. And back home in Europe? There is no mystery here. The Templars became cash-rich, creditworthy, well-trusted, international and immensely experienced in financial management; and so they became important. In the drama of the Knights Templar, their rise and fall, Mary Magdalene plays no part.

10

Why Were the Templars Suppressed?

The Templars were a religious order whose brothers were warriors and bankers. So far, so good. But none of this can answer the last and most insistent question: If the order was central to the life and ideals of Europe, why was it suppressed?

We will never know for sure. Not because we can find no reasons; on the contrary, we can find too many.

Philip IV of France was chronically short of money. His father had built up vast debts on a failed crusade; Philip himself went to war with England and Flanders. Again and again he had to debase his currency. In 1291 he seized the property of the Italian bankers. In 1296 he exacted money from the clergy and so provoked a confrontation with the Pope. In 1306 he confiscated the property of the Jews. In the same year he declared that the coinage would be restored to the standards set by his grandfather Louis IX. It was easy to promise, almost impossible to achieve. Philip needed gold and silver for minting. Where could he find it? In 1307 he turned his attention to the Templars, their lands and their treasure.

Was cash his only motive? Perhaps not. Philip was conspicuously devout, to the point (we might say) of being superstitious. He revered Louis IX, the great crusader who had been canonized in 1297 thanks to the efforts of Philip himself. Throughout his reign Philip attacked or punished those, even in his own family, who seemed to be threatening his realm – and God's protection of his realm – by their impiety. He and his agent Nogaret even kidnapped the Pope and accused him of sodomy, heresy, unbelief and consultations with a private demon. How eerie it will be, to hear similar charges lodged against the Templars. When the inquisitors examined the Templars' Visitor of France (the Grand Master's own representative), he confessed to an astonishing array of crimes. Here is an extract from Barber and Bate (2002, pp. 254–5):

Asked about the manner of the receptions [into the Order] he said on his oath that after the candidates had promised to observe the statutes and the secrets of the Order . . . he led them to some secret place. There he made them kiss him at the bottom of the spine, on the navel and on the mouth, and then had brought before them a cross and told them that the statutes of the Order required them to deny the Crucified one and the cross three times, to spit upon the cross and the image of Jesus Christ, the Crucified one; although this is what he ordered them to do, he did not do this with his heart . . .

Asked about the head, previously mentioned, he said on his oath that he had seen it, held it and stroked it at Montpellier in a chapter-meeting, and he and other brothers present had adored [*adoraverunt*] it with his lips, not with his heart and then only in pretence . . . Asked where it might be, he said that he sent it to Brother Peter Alemandin, preceptor of the house at Montpellier, but did not know if the king's men had found it. He said that this head had four feet, two at the front, under the face, and two behind.

He said on his oath that he said to those he received that if any heat of nature were to incite them to break their chastity, he gave them permission to relieve the pressure with other brothers, although he did this only with his lips, not with his heart.

So much for the Templars' self-presentation as Christendom's most dedicated defenders! Have we found at last the truth behind their well-crafted façade? Robert Langdon recalled the tales of the Templars' strange, secretive rituals; and here they are, publicly described by the most powerful Templar in France. Did the Templars deny Christ because they knew he was a man like any other, and no god? Did that 'head' enclose a relic, to be venerated (rather than worshipped) for proving the truth about Jesus and Mary Magdalene?

For all their power and prestige, the Templars were, in many ways, an easy target for the king. By the 1260s a poet – himself a Templar – could already write in despair of the Muslims' victories over the crusaders: 'Alas, the losses in Syria have been so heavy that its power is dispersed for ever. Then it is really foolish to fight the Turks, now that Jesus Christ no longer opposes them. Daily they impose new defeats on us; for God, who used to watch on our behalf, is now asleep, and Bafometz [that is, Muhammad] puts forth his power to support the Sultan.'

In 1291 Acre, the last of the Latin strongholds on the Syrian mainland, was captured and sacked by the Muslim enemy. For a while the Templars maintained a presence in the East, where they could: they sent troops to Cyprus in 1297, but failed to co-ordinate with the rest of the Western army; they fortified and held the island of Ruad, just off the Syrian coast, but that too was captured in 1302. And so the Templars' work in the East was at an end. The crusades had promised so much; and all of it – maintained for so long at such vast expense – had crumbled to nothing. God had not fought for his own soldiers nor, through them, for his own Holy Land. How could God possibly have abandoned them – unless they had first abandoned him? Christian Europe had good reason to be frightened by the loss of the Holy Land – and of the evil within Christendom itself which had undermined the crusaders' work and brought God's anger down upon it.

What role did the Templars now have in the Church's life? They ran no hospitals; they drained resources and authority from local dioceses; their leaders (now based in Cyprus) kept scant control of the houses on the continent of Europe, which they hardly ever visited. The Templars' enemies had accused them for over a century of insatiable greed. A poem written around 1300 makes only too clear how deeply the Templars were by then resented (from Partner, 1981, p. 36):

> Since many Templars now disport themselves on this side of the sea, riding their grey horses or taking their ease in the shade and admiring their own fair locks, – tell me, why the Pope continues to tolerate them at all. Tell me why he permits them to misuse the riches which are offered them for God's service, on dishonourable and even criminal ends. It is a pity we do not rid ourselves of them for good!

To be rid of the Templars for good: that is exactly what Philip IV of France set out to achieve.

What should an innocent defendant do when on trial for his life? Surely he should protest his innocence and do all he can to prove it? In the French inquisitions, Templar after Templar simply confessed. Even their greatest admirers among us must begin to blanche in the face of such evident and undisputed guilt.

But let's pause. We readily envisage, at these trials, a cool, calm deposition to the inquisitors, duly recorded by their notaries and sent on to the central authorities for the gradual construction of an ever fuller (and, as it turned out, an ever more damning) picture overall. That might have made for a fair, open-minded enquiry – but was not what Philip IV had in mind at all. In September 1307 he had sent secret orders to his bailiffs throughout the kingdom. On a set date, they must detain all Templars for crimes 'horrible to contemplate, terrible to hear of, a heinous crime, an execrable evil, an abominable deed, a hateful disgrace'. The king wanted all those involved in the trials to be quite clear before they began: the Templars were guilty.

The king insisted he had at first been incredulous of the charges; further investigation, however, made them more plausible. And 'the deeper and fuller the investigation has become, the greater are the abominations that are uncovered'; the king therefore was launching an investigation under the Dominican William of Paris, papal inquisitor in northern France and the king's own confessor. It was for the Pope to control such inquisitions, but William of Paris – the king emphasized – had 'invoked the help of [the royal] arm in this matter'. The king had been glad to oblige.

The Templars: Guilty until Proved Innocent!

The king's letter summarized the order's crimes: At a knight's reception into the order, the knight had to deny Christ and spit on a crucifix, each three times. He was then kissed, by the Visitor or the Visitor's deputy, on the base of the spine, on the navel and on the mouth. The kiss on the mouth was a reputable gesture, familiar from other initiations; the other kisses could well be described, in the king's words, as a 'disgrace to the dignity of the human race'. The knights were, from the time of their reception, obliged to accept the sexual advances of any brother Templar.

The Visitor of France, of whom we have already heard, would be confessing to charges drawn up in detail before the formal investigation even began.

The king also issued full instruction to the bailiffs, as follows (from Barber and Bate, 2002, pp. 244–8).

They will place the persons individually under separate and secure guard, and will investigate them first before calling the commissioners of the enquiry, and will determine the truth carefully, with the aid of torture if necessary, and if these persons confess the truth, they will put their depositions in writing to be witnessed.

All this was to be done by the local bailiffs, prior to any interviews by the king's commissioners. Torture could be used, to get the right answers. We well know, in our generation, how much can be achieved as well by passive torture: by solitary confinement; by the threat of violence; by the open presumption of guilt.

Procedure for the enquiry: The articles of the faith will be impressed upon them and they will be told that the King and the Pope have been informed by several trustworthy witnesses in the Order of the errors and the buggery [*bougrerie*] they commit particularly on their entry and their profession. They will be promised a pardon if they confess the truth and return to the faith of the holy Church; otherwise they will be condemned to death.

Then the errors are listed, as in the king's letter from which we have already heard. We hear of one more: each brother wears a cord around his waist.

> It is said that these small cords have been touched and put around an idol in the form of a man's head with a large beard, which head they kiss and adore [*baisent et aourent*] in their provincial chapters; however, not all the brothers are aware of this, only the Grand Master and the elders.

Unbelief, sodomy, heresy and demon-worship: here again were the accusations which the king and Nogaret had laid against the Pope. The Templars' ceremonies of reception were notoriously secret, and gave scope to tireless and shocking rumours; Nogaret would take full advantage of them.

On Friday 13 October 1307 every Templar house in France was occupied by the king's officers. On 14 October Nogaret assembled a group of dignitaries at Notre-Dame and described the charges. On Sunday 15 October Dominicans and royal officials took up the theme, before a larger crowd. The propaganda was under way.

The Templars were threatened with torture from the start. There was the rack, which stretched the limbs and dislocated the joints. There was the strappado: a rope tied the victim's hands behind his back, and was slung over a high beam; he was hauled up into the air and allowed to plummet downwards, to stop a few inches from the ground. Or, simplest of all, the victim's feet could be coated in fat and fixed in front of an open fire to fry. Most of those arrested were the managers, craftsmen and workers of the Templars' French estates; these were not soldiers, hardened against pain by war. A defendant who continued obdurate – and whose guilt was assumed from the start – would most likely be burnt at the stake. To say what the accusers wanted was to save one's life; to deny it was to condemn oneself to torture and, almost certainly, to a terrible death. The accused had every motive to admit to their guilt and, minimizing their own penance, to pass the blame upwards to the order's leaders. Not every Templar confessed to every charge. But the king had prepared his ground well; his agents got more than enough of the answers they wanted.

Within a few weeks the king had secured the most important confessions: above all, from the Grand Master himself, Jacques de Molay. On 25 and 26 October de Molay and other leaders repeated their confessions in public. De Molay then wrote open letters to exhort all other Templars to confess. On 9 November the Visitor of France made his confession from which we have already heard. He was asked whether other leaders received brothers with the same denials of Christ and ritualized kissing that he had required of his candidates? At first he said he did not know. But later on the same day, the notaries recorded, he corrected that answer: now he stated his opinion that all brothers were received in the same way. We can only suspect that torture had been threatened or applied; the king's agents needed this grandee to inculpate the order as a whole, not just himself. The Visitor was asked, in conclusion, a standard question asked of all defendants: whether he had made any of his statement 'because of threats or fear of torture or imprisonment'. No, he said, he had not. We do not know how many people believed it at the time; nobody believes it now.

Could the charges laid against the Templars possibly have been well founded? Well, we say there's no smoke without fire. The king and Pope had heard such rumours about the order by 1305 and had discussed them; by spring 1307 the Templars were moving up the king's agenda; in August the Pope announced a commission to investigate the rumours. But we are bound to wonder, how reliable was the information that actually led to the arrests? The few informants whose identity we know do not inspire confidence. One wrote to the King of Aragon claiming the reward which, he said, the king had promised him (probably in 1305). Others were disaffected Templars who wanted to leave the order; and the King of France was said to have set spies to enter the order, find out what they could and then leave. All will have known what Philip wanted to hear.

Can the Templars' confessions, extracted under such conditions, possibly be trusted? One very distinguished historian suspects, against the current tide of scholarship, that there were houses in France in which knights *were* expected, at their reception, to deny Christ and to blaspheme the cross; that some knights had been horrified by the ritual (and had, if sufficiently insistent and influential, been spared it) – and that there were senior members of the order who were turning a blind eye to the scandal.

But more than that? We might well be intrigued by that image of a demon and its adoration. But no such image was ever found in any Templar house. The stories are a fantasy, linking the head-reliquaries familiar at the time with an imaginary 'Baphomet'; his name was a corruption of 'Muhammad'. The Templars had several head-reliquaries, including (it was believed) one of St Euphemia and perhaps one of their founder, Hugh of Payns. (To adore, *adorare*, a saint's relic was not idolatry; adoration was offered to saints and was distinct from the worship offered only to God.)

The king's agents had stage-managed the whole affair with consummate skill. He must have expected the order to collapse in a cloud of shame. But it didn't. Further confessions certainly followed. The Templars spoke in mortal fear and told the inquisition whatever they thought the king wanted to be told. Their stories took ever more varied forms and became ever more elaborate. The demon's image, according to these confessions, was sometimes a painting of the demon's head, sometimes a statue of this head (variously described as a skull, as white, as black or as having three faces), once a small full-length figurine, sometimes the image of a cat (a classic accomplice of witchcraft). The homoerotic rituals were now re-imagined as orgies with young women.

But the Pope and the other kings of Europe did not

trust the charges or the confessions. Defendants who won access to the Pope's agents – away from the king's – described their torture and insisted on their innocence. The Templars rallied, and it took six years of political manoeuvring – and a few judicial murders – for the King of France finally to get his way. Right to the end, the Templars managed to embarrass him. On 18 March 1314 a commission of cardinals, appointed by the Pope, convened in Paris to pass judgement on four remaining leaders: among them the Grand Master Jacques de Molay and the Visitor of France. On such a papal commission these defendants had always pinned their hopes for an acquittal. It was not to be. They were sentenced 'to harsh and perpetual imprisonment'. For de Molay, an old man who now saw all vindication at an end, this was too much. He announced to the commission and the attendant grandees that his confessions had been false. This was wholly unexpected. The commissioners were non-plussed; they postponed judgement to the next day, and handed over de Molay for safe-keeping to King Philip IV's chief officer in Paris.

Before nightfall the king had commanded de Molay's instant execution; he was taken out to a small island in the Seine and burnt to death. His order effectively died with him; the Templars were at an end.

Part 5
Jesus: Man, God or Gnostic Saviour?

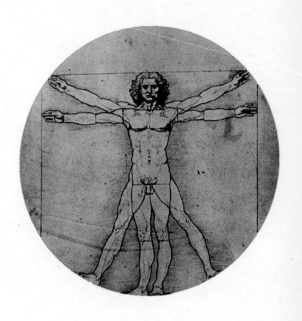

II

From Man to God?
The Story of the Story of Jesus

The centuries are falling away; we are heading back to the fourth century – nearly three hundred years after Jesus died. Here we encounter the Emperor Constantine, master (from 312 CE) of the whole Roman Empire. He decides to unite his subjects under a single religion: Christianity. And so the question looms large: Did Constantine declare Jesus to be God?

Leigh Teabing outlines the achievement of Constantine. Here, abbreviated, is Teabing's account. Jesus Christ was a figure of staggering influence, perhaps the most enigmatic and inspiring leader the world has ever seen. Three centuries after his crucifixion, his followers had multiplied exponentially. Constantine decided something had to be done. He could see that Christianity was on the rise, and he simply backed the winning horse. He needed to strengthen the new Christian tradition, and held a famous ecumenical gathering known as the Council of Nicaea. Until that moment in history, Jesus was viewed by his followers as a mortal prophet, a great and powerful man, but a man nonetheless. A mortal. Jesus' establishment as 'the Son of God' was officially proposed and voted on by the Council of Nicaea.

Is this right? To find out, we need to head back further still, to the first decades after Jesus lived and died. Jesus was Jewish. So were all his first disciples; so was the apostle Paul. It was the great principle of Judaism that there was one God and one only; God is to be worshipped, as is nothing and nobody else. God says, in the book of the prophet Isaiah, 'I am God, and there is none other; for every knee shall bow to me, and every tongue shall confess God' (Isaiah 45.22–23).

In the 50s or 60s CE – 30 years at most after the death of Jesus – Paul wrote to his converts in the city of Philippi. In his letter he quoted a hymn: perhaps one that he had written himself, perhaps one he had inherited. He seems to expect his converts in Philippi to recognize the hymn; perhaps, then, he taught it to them on his own visit to the city, some five years before.

The hymn is in two parts. The first speaks of Jesus' willingness to humble himself: 'he made himself empty, being born in the likeness of humans; he humbled himself and was obedient to the point of death – and death on a cross'. And in the hymn's second part Jesus is rewarded for his obedience: 'Therefore God has highly exalted him and has given him the name above every name, so that at the name of Jesus every knee shall bow' (from Philippians 2.6–10). Every knee shall bow at the name of Jesus: *within 30 years of his death, Jesus was being given the worship that could be given to God alone.* Of all the startling things in early Christianity, this is the most remarkable of all.

It was indeed under Constantine, in the fourth century, that the churches' leaders defined in the terms of Greek philosophy what status this Jesus had in relation to God himself. But the instinct was there from the earliest decades: Jesus must be worshipped as God alone is worshipped. Such worship, in itself, raises more questions than it answers; and it would be 300 years before the churches' thinkers had worked through all the possible implications (and hazards!) of all the possible accounts they could give of this Jesus. Constantine required his bishops to endorse one such view, expressed in sophisticated and carefully ambiguous language. And why was a formulation – *this* formulation – needed just *then*? Did the emperor coolly calculate what would serve his imperial aims? No. The churches were in crisis, and only the emperor could resolve it.

In 318 CE a dispute broke out in the churches that would blaze or smoulder for a century. A brilliant teacher named Arius, in Alexandria in Egypt, proposed a view of Jesus Christ that was based in Scripture, logical and, to anyone trained in Greek thought, reassuringly credible. It went as follows.

There is one perfect and utterly transcendent God: he alone is eternal, wise, and ruler of all. He is the source and origin of everything that is created. There can be no question of his sharing his divine essence with anyone else.

So who or what was Christ? He was created by God to be the agent of God. He was, as Paul had said, the first-begotten of all creation (Colossians 1.15), and so was part of creation. To use the slogan ascribed to Arius: 'There was when Christ was not.' Christ the Son, then, is finite, and can have no real knowledge of the infinite Father; so he can relay to us no real knowledge of that Father. The Son was morally impeccable; but only by his own resolute will. This will bore him through suffering and death – from which God must clearly be immune. This Jesus may be many things; but he must be wholly distinct from God. What stirred Arius into this polemic? Claims which were already being made for Jesus and which Arius was determined to refute.

Who knows the name Arius now? He is almost forgotten. But there are, I suspect, a great many informal Arians within and around the churches today. Such people respect – even revere – Jesus; they regard him as a perfect person and (in practice and probably in principle) unique. Arius delved into the details of the Son's relation to the Father, as many modern Arians do not. But his clarity seems refreshing, and can seem far less confusing today than the churches' later claims that Jesus was wholly God and wholly human.

Arius stirred up a storm. Just as Constantine was strengthening the churches as a power for unity and cohesion in his Empire, Arius was splitting those churches themselves down the middle. Constantine sought – and more or less demanded – unity at Nicaea among the Christian theologians who were effectively in his service. He won the agreement he wanted: of the 220 bishops at the Council, 218 signed their agreement to the creed that Constantine proposed.

The agreement was clearly constructed from an earlier document. I have put in italics the clauses that are likely to have been inserted at the Council to rebut the claims of Arius. The Council was not inventing a claim that Jesus was God. Far from it. The Council was defending that claim – however hard it was to define it in detail – against a powerful attack. Here is the creed on which the bishops agreed:

> We believe in one God, the Father, almighty,
> maker of all things visible and invisible.

There was, then, no question of there being a great God and then a lesser, deceptive god responsible for the material world. We shall see, in the next chapters, why the bishops needed to make this so clear.

> And in one Lord Jesus Christ, the Son of God,
> Begotten from the Father, only-begotten –
> *that is, from the substance of the Father –*
> *God from God, light from light,*
> *True God from true God,*
> *Begotten not made,*
> *Of the same substance with the Father.*

The term 'substance', *ousia*, bore many meanings. (It still does.) The ambiguities of the word turned out to be its great strength – different factions could agree that the Son is *of the same substance with the Father* without necessarily agreeing what it meant.

The creed continued. To make sure there was no wriggling-room for Arians, the meaning of those vital lines was clarified in a further paragraph:

> *But as for those who say, 'There was when he was not,' and 'Before being born he was not,' and 'He came into existence out of nothing,' or who assert that 'The Son of God is a different substance, or is subject to alteration or change' – these the universal and apostolic church declares to be accursed.*

The main body of this creed has a familiar ring to it. Christians still recite a version of it, only lightly amended, in services today. But its victory was not assured by the agreement at Nicaea. The Arians regrouped, and within 50 years had swept all before them. The allegiance of successive emperors – and the outcome of wars between them – was crucial. It would take a further counter-attack, political as much as theological, to restore the Nicene formula to the centre of the churches' life.

Leigh Teabing claims that a single declaration turned Jesus, in the Empire's propaganda, from a man into a god. No. Within a few decades of Jesus' death, the New Testament recorded that worship was being given to Jesus that could be given to God alone. Where that first generation of Christians led, all future generations of Christians would follow: such worship, they were sure, was owed to Jesus. This posed the greatest question to confront the thinkers of the early churches: who could – or must – that Jesus have been, to be entitled to that worship? The struggle among theologians to define Jesus' true standing was a struggle that, at Nicaea, still had 100 years to run. Jesus: man or God or both at once? To find an answer, Teabing shines a spotlight on a single Council, in 325 CE; and leaves in darkness, all around it, 400 years of agonized thought and daily devotion.

Let's turn the beam of light backwards, to illumine two earlier moments in this struggle. In the first, the Gnostics will take centre-stage. Dan Brown's characters are right to stress the Gnostics' importance in the Christian drama of the second and third centuries, but they misread the parts the Gnostics played. And the second moment, more distant still? This is the moment that underlies all the churches' thought about Mary Magdalene. When we reach it, we will have found the origin of every story and the heart of every hope to which Mary Magdalene has given rise. And it is a moment not mentioned by Dan Brown's characters at all. We too, in this short book, have been on a circuitous quest of false leads and dead-ends. Only in our final pages will we reach at last our own Holy Grail: the meeting of Jesus and Mary Magdalene on Easter Day.

The Truth Shall Set You Free:
Becoming Mary Magdalene

'The early Church,' says Teabing, 'needed to convince the world that the mortal prophet Jesus was a *divine* being. Therefore, any gospels that described *earthly* aspects of Jesus had to be omitted from the Bible. Unfortunately for the early editors, one particularly troubling earthly theme kept recurring in the gospels. Mary Magdalene. More specifically, her marriage to Jesus Christ.'

Legend after legend grew and blossomed about Jesus and Mary Magdalene in the second and third centuries CE. Some groups among Jesus' followers, in these years, incorporated Jesus into a strange but compelling story of spirit, soul and physical matter. Their claims were the subject of fierce disputes; divisions in the Church are not new. Some – but only some – of these groups called themselves 'Gnostics'. When we nowadays speak of Gnostics, we are speaking of many different teachers and groups that we (not they) have declared to be a single movement. Teabing tells of the Gnostic gospels discovered at Nag Hammadi in Egypt in the 1940s: in these, he says,

Jesus is spoken of in very human terms. Quite the opposite is true. The Gnostics spoke only of the ethereal Jesus, already risen from the dead; they ignored the Jesus who, according to the churches, had suffered and died. The Gnostic Jesus who loves Mary Magdalene is the heavenly Jesus; he is no human being like you and me.

For the Gnostics, this physical world of ours is a squalid mistake, the work of a minor deity, arrogant, ignorant and afraid of any rivals to his power. Most individuals are so sunk in spiritual sleep that we need, so the Gnostics claimed, to be woken up to the knowledge of who we *really* are. The individual, once woken, longs to be reunited with the realm of the Spirit. That realm is embodied in Jesus, longing to reunite the individual with himself. How could the Gnostics speak of such a mutual yearning for unity and completeness? Only one form of language could be adequate: the language of sexual love.

According to the Gnostics, none of us can find our way to be back at one with the realm of the Spirit without the Saviour's help. To yearn for knowledge is to yearn for the Saviour, the Spirit; to know the Saviour is to know the Spirit in ourselves. This knowledge will unite us with ourselves.

For the Gnostics (as for all philosophers in the ancient world), men were rational, orderly, spiritual and strong, women were emotional, disruptive, earthbound and weak. What name, then, did Gnostics give to the Saviour, the beloved in this longed-for union? Jesus. And what name did they give to the individual, beleaguered in this coarse world and passionate to clasp and receive the Saviour? For some Gnostics, one name stood out, to denote men and women alike: Mary Magdalene.

Some Gnostics developed a ritual of the Bridal Chamber. Was it a celebration of sexual love and union? No, it was a celebration of the spiritual union that would reveal and transcend the sad illusions of bodily, worldly love.

The Gnostics did not stop here. Women had two other indisputable and invaluable qualities: they were life-giving; and they had access to forms of wisdom to which most men were blind. (This wisdom was a powerful version of what we call 'female intuition'.) Any such distinction, drawn so starkly, is of course misleading; each individual is both rational and emotional, orderly and erratic, strong and weak. But such contrasts, however refined, allowed different Gnostics to view women in two different ways: they could emphasize the supposed weaknesses of women; or the strengths of women's insight. Let's follow each of these two routes, in turn.

First: Were women intrinsically and unavoidably weak, earth-bound and emotional? If so, the consequence for the Gnostics was clear: within any individual, the Female had been found wanting, and must be absorbed into the Male; individuals, ran the argument, became the people they should be when they allowed the Male within them to prevail. What, then, must women themselves do to overcome the weaknesses intrinsic to their sex? They must become like men. The most famous of the Gnostic texts is the

Gospel of Thomas: a Coptic translation of a Greek text (which might itself have been translated from Syriac). The Gospel of Thomas turns twice to the relation between the sexes. Here is the Gospel's final saying. In every way, its last word.

> Simon Peter said to them: Let Mary go out from among us, because women are not worthy of the Life. Jesus said: See, I shall lead her, so that I will make her male, that she too may become a living spirit, resembling you males. For every woman who makes herself male will enter the kingdom of Heaven.
>
> *(Gospel of Thomas, Saying 114)*

How strange it is, that in our generation the Gospel of Thomas – so deeply misogynist – has become popular among those most keenly determined to modernize belief and to free it from the churches' dull, patriachal oppression.

But second: What of the power of women to see what men so rarely see? Almost all people – even almost all Christians – were, in the Gnostics' view, blind to the knowledge offered by Jesus. Most dangerous of all were the leaders of the churches who used their power to denigrate the Gnostics themselves. We have seen who took, in some Gnostic stories, the role of the Gnostic, loving and longing for the beloved Jesus, and drawn upwards by Jesus back to the spiritual realms where the Gnostic belongs: Mary Magdalene, the first person to whom Jesus appeared on Easter Day. So who shall take the role of the blind leaders, enemies of the spirit? The male disciples of Jesus.

There were clearly some Gnostic communities whose members recognized the power of prophetic or visionary women; and there were clearly, in or around those communities, powerful men who deeply resented the women's privilege.

Teabing speaks of the Gnostic Gospel of Mary. In it we overhear voices raised in a real dispute of the second or third century CE. Here Mary Magdalene personifies the privileged, prophetic women in these communities; and Simon Peter personifies the resentful men, anxious at this challenge to their power. Jesus commissions his disciples to preach to the gentiles. Then he leaves them. They are frightened. Mary stiffens their resolve:

> Peter said to Mary, 'Sister, we know that the Saviour loved you more than the rest of women. Tell us the words of the Saviour which you remember – which you know, but we do not, nor have we heard them.'

Mary duly relays the teaching of Jesus on the nature of spiritual visions; but she gets no thanks for her pains.

> Andrew answered and said to the brethren, 'Say what you wish to say about what she has said. I at least do not believe that the Saviour said this. For certainly these teachings are strange ideas.' Peter answered and spoke concerning these same things.

He questioned them about the Saviour: 'Did he really speak privately with a woman and not openly to us? Are we to turn about and all listen to her? Did he prefer her to us?'

Then Mary wept and said to Peter, 'My brother Peter, what do you think? Do you think that I have thought this up myself in my heart, or that I am lying about the Saviour?'

Levi answered and said to Peter, 'Peter, you have always been hot-tempered. Now I see you contending against the woman like the adversaries. But if the Saviour made her worthy, who are you indeed to reject her? Surely the Saviour knows her very well. That is why he loved her more than us.'

(Gospel of Mary, second century,
from 10.1–8, 17.7–18.20)

What are we to make of the Gnostics? For Leigh Teabing in *The Da Vinci Code*, the Gnostics alone preserved the memory of the human Jesus who lived and who loved and who knew the value of women. On the contrary. Some Gnostic groups did defy the conventions of the ancient world – and of the patriarchal churches – and acknowledged the special gifts of knowledge with which the prophetic women in their communities, their Mary Magdalenes, were endowed. Other such groups imagined every Gnostic, male and female, as a Mary Magdalene, intimately bound in knowledge and love with the heavenly Jesus. But no such Magdalenes glorified sexual love; they transcended it. Teabing encourages Sophie: in the

Gnostic records she will find an open enjoyment of sex. No, she won't.

Whatever happened bodily in this world was, for a Gnostic, only a shadow, cast by the real drama of the spirit. The Gnostics' Saviour did not save this physical world; he saved the Gnostic *from* this world. The Gnostics thought deeply, what is it to be human? They asked, 1,800 years ago, searching questions about the Male and Female which we in the modern world have only recently learnt to ask again. Such Gnostics stand as an inspiration. But they stand as a warning too. They asked powerful questions; and reached dark, world-denying answers.

It was not just the Gnostics who asked those questions. The larger churches asked them too; and within those churches some leaders came to answers, different but just as dark and, over the course of centuries, far more damaging.

13

Women in the Early Churches

These larger churches shared with the Gnostics a foundational text: the biblical stories of creation. You may well know them – the stories of creation in six days and of the Fall of Adam and Eve. Adam followed the lead of Eve. This was, for the early churches, surely an inversion of the proper, God-given order of things. God condemned Adam for his weakness: 'Because you have listened to the voice of your wife, and eaten the forbidden fruit – cursed is the ground because of you!' (Genesis 2.17).

Our Bibles include in the New Testament two 'Letters of Paul to Timothy'. It is widely recognized now that the First Letter is by a follower of Paul, not by Paul himself; for centuries, however, the First Letter had all the authority of the great apostle himself:

I permit no woman to teach or to have authority over men; she is to keep silent. For Adam was formed first, then Eve; and Adam was not deceived, but the woman was deceived and became a transgressor. Yet woman will be saved through bearing children, if she continues in faith and love and holiness, with modesty.

(1 Timothy 2.12–15)

This author is battening down the hatches. He wants a steady, respectable, patriarchal church and family life to be maintained. But he has built his instruction on a view of women which could readily turn into vitriolic fear.

In the churches of the second century, in North Africa, some young women decided to remain unmarried. With the encouragement of their fellow-believers, they attended church with their heads unveiled. They may even have been given a place of special prominence in the room, to show their freedom from a woman's sexual life and from the shame attached to it. Christ had come to bring freedom from sin to the women themselves and to all believers. To such women and their allies, the women's guiltless freedom in worship was both an example and a symbol of the great freedom in which Christ's followers lived.

Not everyone agreed. To the church leader Tertullian, the women were shamelessly imitating the temptress Eve. Into the Eden of the Church the serpent had come again. Tertullian fought fiercely for marriage and family life and steadiness. He fought just as fiercely against the dangers that women posed. Did women want to wear attractive clothes and keep their heads uncovered? If only, says Tertullian, you women realized who and what you really are:

None of you at all, best beloved sisters, would have desired too cheerful a style of dress. You would have desired to go about in humble clothes, walking about as Eve, mourning and repentant, in order that by every garment of penitence you might the more fully expiate what you derive from Eve: The ignominy, I mean, of the first sin, and the odium of human perdition. In pains and in anxieties do you bear children, woman; and toward your husband is your inclination, and he lords it over you (adapted from Genesis 3.16).

Do you not know that you are each an Eve? The sentence of God on this sex of yours lives on in this age; the guilt must of necessity live on too. *You* are the devil's gateway; *you* are the unsealer of that forbidden tree; *you* are the first deserter of the divine law; *you* are she who persuaded the man whom the devil was not brave enough to attack. *You* destroyed so easily God's image, man. On account of the death that *you* deserved, even the Son of God had to die.

(Tertullian, *On the Apparel of Women* I.1.1–2)

This tradition has bequeathed to the churches a legacy of terrible convictions, infected by men's fear, their guilt and the grip they want to keep on power. The churches could teach a dark but simple symmetry: the first Eve had brought about the Fall; and her daughters still bore her guilt. Eve had *seduced* Adam, and all Adam's sons were still in danger from such seduction by the daughters of Eve.

A first Eve, in this tradition, brought about the Fall.

A second Eve must undo it. At the heart of the human Fall was sex, fatally abused; at the heart of human restoration must be sex, forgiven for its past and freed from all abuse. That restoration was under way in the life, death, rising – and churches – of Jesus. In the Christian story, the part of the second Eve is played by Jesus' mother, the Blessed Virgin Mary, through a conception – and even a whole life – free from sin. To be free from sin was above all to be free from sexual contamination. In our ongoing world of marriage and procreation, a sexually active woman could not model herself on the Blessed Virgin. She could at best subject herself to the will – and not least, to the sexual will – of her husband, her own Adam. Woman, once weak enough to be seduced by the serpent, must have no opportunity to be seduced or to seduce again. And Man, whose role is to lead, must ensure by all possible means that he is not led astray again by any woman. Such ideas have led to a frightened, cruel misogyny that has defaced all Christendom.

St Augustine, greatest of all the Latin Fathers, emphasized that after the Fall Adam and Eve, in their embarrassment, covered their genitals. 'Look,' he exclaimed, 'that's the place from which the first sin is passed on' (Augustine, Sermon 151.5). Sexual feeling, claimed Augustine, is a penalty for disobedience, and urges us to disobedience; it is a 'torture of the will'. It is only fitting that the taint of original sin should be passed on within the process of reproduction itself, from the guilty Adam through all generations. 'Sin entered the world', says Paul, according to

Augustine's (inaccurate) translation, 'through one man, . . . in whom all sinned' (Romans 5.12). The Western Church has followed Augustine: precisely within sexual desire and activity lies the dreadful, ineradicable root of evil; we can no more free ourselves from the power of evil than we can free ourselves from the sexual instinct that stirs that evil within us. But Jesus? Born of a virgin mother, he was free from that inherited miasma that infects the rest of us; and he remained free from the disobedience which that miasma stirs and represents.

Time and again, we have watched Dan Brown's characters misread the past. But on this most important theme of all, they see the churches' early history more clearly than many of us do, even now, within the churches themselves.

It may unsettle – but should not surprise – today's churches that many people would like to 'rescue' Jesus from the churches' grasp, and in particular to decontaminate him from his followers' obsession with the darker side of sex. Attention turns to Jesus himself: was he married? The Bible says nothing about it, either way; and it is very rare indeed for a Jewish man to be unmarried. So Teabing and Langdon can explain to Sophie: 'Jesus as a married man makes infinitely more sense than our standard biblical view of Jesus as a bachelor . . . If Jesus were not married, at least one of the Bible's gospels would have mentioned it, and offered some explanation for his unnatural state of bachelorhood.'

Can we then conclude that Jesus himself was most likely married?

14

Jesus: A Believable Bachelor?

Wait just a moment, before we come to our decision. There is a thin but bright scarlet thread of celibacy to be followed through the Judaism of Jesus' day – and in the very circles around Jesus himself. To be chaste was central to some special tasks and some special ways of life. First, soldiers fighting God's wars had to be chaste on active service. And second, priests had to be chaste in their periods of service in the Temple in Jerusalem; in part, because the Temple was the presence on earth of heaven itself, the court of God. To be in the Temple, then, was to be in heaven. Creatures of heaven were immortal and needed no children; they were celibate. It is no wonder, then, that the priests on duty – temporary creatures of heaven – were chaste.

As in Jerusalem, so at the other 'Temple' of which Jesus will have known. The sectarians at Qumran, site of the Dead Sea Scrolls, saw themselves as soldiers in the vanguard of God's battle against his people's enemies. They saw themselves, too, as priests. Out in the desert, far from the Temple in Jerusalem, their community *was* the Temple, true to God's law which the priests in Jerusalem had betrayed. The Qumran-ites were, then, priests living *as* their Temple and on permanent duty within it. So they were living some part of the life of heaven, and – as we would expect – they were celibate.

The Qumranites had a clear influence on John the Baptist, the prophet who lived in the desert and proclaimed the coming of God's dominion. We hear of the Baptist from the biblical Gospels and from the Jewish historian Josephus, active towards the end of the first century CE. The Baptist seems likely – living as he did – to have been celibate.

The Baptist was the teacher (and according to Luke, the cousin) of Jesus. So it would, at the least, be no surprise if Jesus himself had been celibate too. We hear how he demanded that his followers value himself, his name and the gospel above any family ties. Mark, Matthew and Luke all have Jesus promise rewards for those who leave their children. Luke (and only Luke) has him speak as well of those who leave – or even 'hate' – their wife (Luke 14.26, 18.29); such a Jesus, we may think, must surely have been single himself or have left his wife behind.

It remains *possible* that Jesus was married. Although he was clearly influenced by ascetic teachers, in some ways he clearly reacted against them (Matthew 11.18–19). We will never be sure whether he learnt from those teachers how to be celibate – or turned against their teachings and was (for some part of his adult life?) a married man.

My own suspicion, as a historian, is that Jesus was celibate. You may, though – and perhaps with good reason, – distrust my claim to the detachment of a historian. I am marinated in Christian history, tradition and thought; I have a heavy investment (even heavier than I myself may recognize) in the familiar claims about Jesus. Am I really the person to mount a proper, disinterested historical argument about him?

It is as well to be aware what is at stake. How would Christian thought change if it were ever to be believed by the churches that Jesus was married? Imagine the dignity that would be given to sexual relations; and the challenge to any rule on priestly celibacy. Imagine, as well, the muddle that would follow over the status of Jesus' wife and the nature of their children; we would have to re-imagine the relation between 'mere' humans and the descendants of Jesus, and so the relation between being-human and being-God, – and so the definition of Jesus himself. How differently we would view the virginal mother of Jesus; how soon we would be wondering whether the imbalance in favour of the Male should be redressed within our understanding of God himself.

Uproar. It will never happen. But before any such thought-experiment is decried for an obsession with sex, let's look across to Judaism, ancient and modern. Judaism has been spared some of the intellectual and imaginative agonies of the Christian churches: Judaism has never credited any God-man such as Jesus; and has not needed to define the status of his mother or explore its consequences – let alone the status of his wife and children. Judaism has simply got on with marriage and with sex within it. In daily life and in the stories of all its greatest heroes Judaism continues to respect the first commandment which God gave to the first man and first woman: 'Be fruitful and multiply' (Genesis 1.28). Has this led, within Judaism, to centuries of sexual immorality? On the contrary. Judaism was already famous in the Roman Empire for its profound personal and social morality, and is still famous for it today.

Jesus: married or single? The argument will run and run. The fight over his marriage – and so his sexual activity – is a small battle in a far larger campaign. Teabing wants to remove all the baroque decoration of divinity that the churches have piled on to the figure of Jesus, and reveal him as the human being he was. To do so, he allies himself with the Gnostics. But he has joined the wrong army. It was the Gnostics who omitted from their texts all reference to the earthly Jesus. The larger churches insisted, with brutal clarity, that Jesus was an earthly, human being: *he died.*

15

'Crucify Him! Crucify Him!'

And what a vile death it was.

We have heard the story of Jesus' Last Supper with his closest friends and pupils; and of his prediction that one of them was about to betray him. The story is about to get as dark as the night it is set in.

Judas Iscariot, the traitor, has gone to Jesus' enemies. He knows where Jesus will be going. These enemies waste no time. They head off to the garden. But it will be dark there; Jesus will be among his other disciples. How are the soldiers to know which is Jesus, and to be sure of arresting him before he can get away? Judas has given them a signal: he will go up to Jesus himself, and greet him with a kiss. So he will betray his teacher and friend.

Jesus does not resist. Peter draws his sword and cuts off the ear of one adversary; but Jesus stops the fight, and heals the wounded man. Jesus' disciples run away. Overnight, Jesus is questioned. The next morning he is presented to the crowds. They bay for his blood: 'Crucify him! Crucify him!' He is condemned to death: to be stripped of his clothes, hung up on a wooden cross for all to see, and left to die. Two further troublemakers, we are told, were also due to be killed. The three of them could be dealt with together. We know from other reports the details of such public executions; the Gospels' first readers would have known them far better.

Whipped and beaten, already faint from loss of blood, condemned men were made to carry the wooden beams from which they would be hung. The victims were led to a bleak patch of rising ground outside the city's wall. Here was the regular site for executions: a series of posts stood out against the sky, eight feet high; into the top of each was cut a notch.

The routine was familiar. Nothing marked out this set of crucifixions from the last. Sometimes rope was used to fix the prisoner to the cross, sometimes nails. There is an ancient tradition that Jesus was nailed.

The beam was laid on the ground. The soldiers put Jesus on to his back across the beam and along it stretched out his arms. First one hand, then the other: a soldier would press the back of Jesus' hand against the beam, hold a nail to the wrist and drive it home, through pulse and bone, to the wood behind. The soldiers lifted the beam's ends on to two forked poles, hoisted the beam and Jesus into the air, and slotted the beam's centre into the notch at the top of the post.

Now for the feet. Each of Jesus' ankles was sandwiched between a block of wood and the side of the upright post. From each side a nail was hammered in.

And there Jesus would hang, for as long as it took him to die.

It was an infamously, spectacularly cruel form of execution. It was used for rebels and runaway slaves. The longer they lasted, the better. A stool might be attached to the post, on which the victim could rest; his circulation would revive, his suffering would be prolonged. So much the better, too, that the mob could see what became of troublemakers; here was a warning to anyone else who might dare oppose the might of Rome. A condemned criminal carried a placard stating the charge on which the Roman authorities had convicted him. Jesus' placard was hung above him on the cross, to mock the pretensions of his followers: 'Jesus of Nazareth, the king of the Jews.'

What about those friends of Jesus, the men who had made such a fuss of their loyalty and courage at the Last Supper – where were they? Not where they were needed. Only the Beloved Disciple was there to see Jesus die; all the rest had run away.

And the women who had been linked with Jesus? *They* were there. The different Gospels identify them differently. Among them were the mother of Jesus (John 19.25); and Mary, the wife of Clopas (John 19.26), who is likely to have been the Mary who was the mother of James and Joseph (Matthew 27.56; Mark 15.40).

But one Mary is mentioned, unambiguously, by Matthew, Mark and John: Mary Magdalene.

16

Back to Eden:
Jesus and Mary Magdalene

Our journey through Christian history is near its end.
Do Robert Langdon and Leight Teabing – and Dan
Brown himself – show us the truth about centuries of
conspiracies and lies, all protecting the churches and
in particular the Church of Rome? No. There have
been, in Christian history, more than enough conspiracies and lies and errors; but those imagined in
The Da Vinci Code are not among them.

Dan Brown's instinct, nonetheless, is spot-on.
Whatever the churches may say, they look wealthy,
powerful, authoritarian and dominated by men. If
they really cannot see or admit how badly they have
treated women in the past, there is little hope for a
change in that treatment in the future.

Mary Magdalene has suffered, in her reputation,
more than most. The Church confused her with
another woman, apparently a prostitute, who encountered Jesus; and so Mary Magdalene herself was
stigmatized for centuries as a whore. Women were
offered two role-models from the Bible: the Blessed
Virgin Mary, virginal mother of Jesus who was never

besmirched by sexual activity; and Mary Magdalene, who repented of her trade and renounced all sexual activity. For the celibate men in charge of the Church had good reason to be frightened by women's sexual appeal; so only those women were safe who had vowed not to use it.

Can we rescue Mary Magdalene from centuries of error and fear? Heading backwards through history, we have at last reached the origin of all the elaborate stories about the love of Jesus and Mary Magdalene. It is the story of Easter morning in John's Gospel. It is not even mentioned by Dan Brown's characters; we must at last leave Robert, Sophie and Teabing behind, and see for ourselves what none of them sees.

To end this short book, I suggest we just hear John's story of Easter. But we need to sort out two preliminaries first.

First: How should we best read this story of Easter? We are inclined to think that we should assess the gospels as we might assess any other text. The Gospels make claims to historical truth; and we have to decide if we believe those claims. But we should beware. Rightly or wrongly, John thought that his Jesus confounds all our normal ways of thought. He *knew* that his claims were enough to make his readers' brains hurt. John, as he himself saw it, was not just showing those readers what to know and think, but enabling them to know and think it.

In the course of John's story Jesus heals, feeds, gives new sight and brings to new life; and what Jesus does in the story, the story is designed to do within John's readers. John takes his readers on a roller-coaster ride. As the characters who encounter Jesus are baffled and teased and cajoled into understanding, so are the readers. John's Jesus tells Nicodemus, at the Gospel's start, of the need for re-birth from above (John 3.3); Nicodemus is utterly bemused. At the mid-point of the story, Jesus actually raises his friend Lazarus, the brother of Martha and Mary, from the dead (John 11). Lazarus is re-born from above. *And John sets out to prepare, to effect or to evoke within his readers, during the reading of his Gospel, just such re-birth from 'the dead'.* The readers who read about Lazarus, born again from above, read about themselves and about the baptism in which they themselves have been or are being or will soon be summoned from the dead to new life. We think of the Gospel as there to be read and studied; but it was really written to be *undergone*.

Character after character meets Jesus, is bemused and challenged and tries to come to understanding; so, in every case, does the reader. The last character we meet is Mary Magdalene. She is loyal to the end: when most of the male disciples have run away, she stays at the foot of the cross and sees Jesus die. Two days later, she is the one who comes to the tomb to tend his body; as the reader might come in imagination, to lament the Jesus who has been betrayed, tortured and killed.

Now John's readers or audience almost certainly knew the story of Jesus in outline before they ever encountered John's immensely sophisticated re-telling of it, and any fully-fledged member of his community was likely to read or hear the Gospel regularly. The

Easter story, then, does not come as a surprise. As an increasingly familiar story, it can evoke what the readers already know about themselves, their bereavements, their mortality – and their 're-birth' at their own baptism. The Easter story stirs up the reader's imagination and sympathy; so that he or she can recognize, in this single unforgettable scene, what such re-birth brings the 're-born' to.

So, is John's story true? I seem to have turned it into a form of poetry – imaginative, evocative, touching – but about as bad a guide to what actually happened as a play by Shakespeare. Well, we need to remember what John is trying to achieve by his Gospel. His readers must be taken, with the help of the Gospel, through the re-birth they need if they are to see the truth of the Gospel; and such readers will recognize themselves in the story of Easter Day.

Yes, yes, you may say, but we still want to know, is the story *true*? John, I think, would say that only the re-born can give a proper answer to that; and their answer will be a resounding *Yes*. So, we will ask, are the re-born supposed to believe that the events of Easter morning actually happened the way he tells of them? Once more, Yes. But (as John would have it) only the re-born have even an inkling of what they are really claiming when they say so. And what about those outside – and inside! – the churches who assess and judge John's story of Easter morning as straightforward evidence of an event no less accessible to normal understanding than this morning's sunrise or the arrival of my latest emails? John would think their assessment quite valueless.

John seeks to draw us through new birth; and so to recognize our re-created selves in the figure of Mary Magdalene on Easter Day. Can we, his modern readers, become part of his project, even if we want to? *Should* we want to? John, it seems, seeks to draw us down from the critical detachment that has helped recent generations to see the errors in so much churchy nonsense from the past. We may well want to close our eyes to John, as a dangerous will-o'-the-wisp. That's our choice. I wonder how you, the reader, will view John's invitation, when we have reached the end of this chapter, of our own grail quest and of John's wonderful story.

And the second preliminary: John's Easter story is not self-contained. It is alive with echoes of other stories, even more ancient, from the Bible.

'In the beginning,' we read in Genesis, 'God created the heaven and the earth. And the earth was invisible and unformed; and darkness was over the deep.' God launches Creation with a word: 'Let there be light' (Genesis 1.1, 3). So the work of the first day, Day One, is under way.

God made the Human, and planted a garden in Eden. He put the Human in the Garden of Eden to work it and keep it (2.8–9, 15). But the Human was alone. God decided to make a helper for him. God formed every beast and every bird, and brought them to the Human to see what he would call them. And whatever the Human called every living creature, that was its name – and so the creation of each creature was complete at last. But there was no creature suitable as a mate for the Human; so God created Eve. Adam and Eve were in Eden; but not for long; the serpent deceived them, and they were expelled.

From one garden to another. A man and woman meet again in a garden in the Song of Songs, a collection of love-songs in the Old Testament. At one point the woman loses her beloved.

Woman:
On my bed at night I sought the man that I love
    with all my soul.
I sought but could not find him.
When I found him that I love with all my soul,
I clasped him and would not let him go,
Not till I had brought him to my mother's house,
To the room where she conceived me!

(Song of Solomon, 3.1–4)

And so to John's story of Easter.

Jesus is killed. Two days pass. The new week begins. On Day One of the week, very early, while it is still dark, Mary Magdalene comes to the garden; she finds the tomb empty. She runs to tell Peter and the Beloved Disciple. They come to the tomb. They see the grave-clothes. The Beloved Disciple believes – simply, it seems, – that the tomb is empty, as Mary had told them. And from this, nothing follows. The disciples simply go home.

Mary stood outside the tomb, weeping. As she wept, she stooped down facing the tomb. And she sees two angels, in white, sitting where the body of Jesus had lain, one where his head had been and one where his feet. And they say to her, 'Woman, why are you weeping?' She says to them: 'Because they have taken my lord, and I do not know where they have put him.'

Mary turns round and sees Jesus standing there, and does not know that it is Jesus. 'Woman,' says Jesus, 'why are you weeping? Who are you looking for?' She thinks he is the gardener and says, 'Sir, if you have taken him away, tell me where you have put him and I will take him away.'

Jesus says to her, 'Mary.' She turns and says to him, in Hebrew, 'Rabbouni' (which means 'Teacher').

Jesus says to her, 'Do not go on touching me; for I am not yet ascended to the father. But go to my brothers and tell them: I am going to my father and your father, to my God and your God.'

(John 20.11–18)

A man and a woman are together in a garden at dawn on a spring morning. The woman is at the tomb of the man she revered and loved; she loved him so much that she wants only to care for his broken body. But the body has been taken away. Has it been stolen? Or removed from this grand tomb and discarded? This Mary Magdalene is *the reader*, taken through the whole story and now reaching its apparently disastrous end.

Mary turns. She sees Jesus. She thinks he is the gardener, set to work the garden and keep it. The sky is brightening. Jesus says, *'Mary.'* He has called her by her name; and her creation is complete. Mary knows Jesus at last; and longs to have him as the human presence that she loves and misses. She reaches out for him. For like the lover in the Song of Songs she has found the one that she loves with all her soul; she takes hold of him and will not let him go. The scene is deeply erotic. But this is not the love that Mary must have for Jesus. He refuses her touch: *'Do not go on touching me'* (John 20.17).

Who are these two, this man and this woman, in a springtime garden at dawn on Day One? They are Adam and Eve. They are together again in Paradise, the garden of Eden; and all creation is made new.

Jesus' closest disciples have seen the empty tomb, 'believed' and gone home; how very sensible, rational, orderly and male. Left behind and disregarded is a woman, inconsolably weeping. She gets everything wrong. She has misunderstood the empty tomb, she looks still for Jesus' body, she fails to know him when he stands before her, she longs for an earthly love and a human touch. But it is not to those knowing disciples that Jesus first appears. It is to Mary. For in her weeping is the voice of love.

By Jesus' tomb, in the grey half-light, Mary Magdalene speaks for the readers of John who have undergone his story as he hoped they would: readers who, themselves, have cried for those they have loved and lost.

Mary's tears are the readers' tears. When Jesus calls Mary by her name, he calls the readers as well by theirs.

'Set me as a seal upon your heart', sings the Song of
  Songs,
'as a seal upon your arm.
For love is strong as death.
Many waters cannot quench love,
neither can the floods drown it.'

(Song of Songs 8.6–7)

Mary Magdalene has found her beloved. So have
John's readers.

The light is rising in Paradise.

Notes for Further Reading

I am grateful to Dr Jan Palmowski, Professor Jonathan Riley-Smith and Father Gerard Sheehan for reading various chapters and for proposing important corrections and improvements. Any errors that remain are of course to be laid at my own door.

I have quoted from Dan Brown, *The Da Vinci Code*, London: Corgi, paperback, 2004; and have quoted and referred to M. Baigent, R. Leigh and H. Lincoln, *The Holy Blood and the Holy Grail*, London: Arrow, 1996, pp. 98, 213, 235.

The Priory of Sion

For the Abbey of St Mary of Mount Sion and of the Holy Spirit (on a site linked both with the end of the Blessed Virgin Mary's life on earth and with the descent of the Holy Spirit at Pentecost), and for the role of its canons:

C. J. M. de Vogüé, *Les Églises de la Terre Sainte*, Paris, 1860, p. 326.

For the Abbey's charter:

M. E.-G. Rey, 'Chartes de l'Abbaye du Mont Sion', *Mémoires de la Société Nationale des Antiquaires de France*, 5th series, VIII, Paris: C. Klincksieck, 1887, pp. 31–56.

For a summary of the modern story:

A. Bernstein, 'The French Confection', in D. Burstein (ed.), *Secrets of the Code*, London: Weidenfeld & Nicolson, 2004, pp. 300–5.

As the money from early book sales came in, those involved in the Priory fell out. One of them later wrote bitterly:

G. de Sède, *Rennes-le-Château*, Paris: Robert Laffont, 1988.

For the links woven between Plantard's earlier ideas and Rennes-le-Château:

P. Smith, 'The Plantard Grail', *Journal of the Pendragon Society*, 1986, XVII, no. 3; an additional note, in the following issue, no. 4; and details on the website www.priory-of-sion.com.

Opus Dei

On Spanish Catholicism:

F. Lannon, *Privilege, Persecution and Prophecy: The Catholic Church in Spain, 1875–1975*, Oxford: Clarendon Press, 1987.

On the prelude to the Spanish Civil War:

S. Ben-Ami, *The Origins of the Second Republic in Spain*, Oxford University Press, 1978.

S. Ben-Ami, *Fascism from Above*, Oxford: Clarendon Press, 1983.

On the politics of religion:

J. M. Sánchez, *Reform and Reaction: The Politico-Religious Background of the Spanish Civil War*, Chapel Hill: University of North Carolina Press, 1964.

J. M. Sánchez, *The Spanish Civil War as a Religious Tragedy*, Notre Dame: University of Indiana Press, 1987.

On the Franco regime:

N. B. Cooper, *Catholicism and the Franco Regime*, London: Sage, 1975.

P. Preston, *Spain in Crisis: The Evolution and Decline of the Franco Regime*, Hassocks: Harvester Press, 1976.

On Josemaría Escrivá:

Escrivá's main works are conveniently collected:

J. Escrivá *The Way, The Furrow, The Forge*, Princeton: Scepter, 1998.

P. Berglar, *Opus Dei: The Life and Work of its Founder, Josemaría Escrivá*, trans. B. Browne, Princeton: Scepter, 1994. A hagiography.

A. Vázquez de Prada, *The Founder of Opus Dei: The Life and Work of Josemaría Escrivá*, Princeton: Scepter, 2001. A hagiography.

J. Estruch, *Saints and Schemers: Opus Dei and its Paradoxes*, trans. E. L. Glick, Oxford University Press, 1995. Scrutinizes the early years in great detail.

For the texts of the *Constitutions*, 1950 and the *Statutes*, 1982:

www.odan.org (I have adapted their translation of the Latin.)

For Cardinal Hume:

A. Howard, *Basil Hume: The Monk Cardinal*, London: Headline, 2005, pp. 128–9, 296.

For Opus Dei, most recently:

J. L. Allen, *Opus Dei*, New York: Doubleday, 2005.

For another movement urging the sanctification of life, and influential on Pope John Paul II, compare:

Stefan Cardinal Wyszynski, *All You Who Labor: Work and the Sanctification of Daily Life*, first published in 1946, now Manchester, New Hampshire: Sophia Institute Press, 1995.

The Templars: In general

M. Barber, *The New Knighthood*, Cambridge University Press, 1994.

In less detail: P. P. Read, *The Templars*, London: Weidenfeld & Nicolson, 1999.

Notes for Further Reading

For a selection of documents in translation:
M. Barber and K. Bate (eds), *The Templars*, Manchester University Press, 2002.

The Templars: Finance

On the Templars' banking:
Classically: L. Delisle, *Mémoire sur les Opérations Financières des Templiers*, Mémoires de l'Institut national de France, Académie des Inscriptions et Belles-Lettres, 33 (ii), 1889.
Augmented by: J. C. Piquet, *Les Banquiers au Moyen Age. Les Templiers*, Paris: Hachette, 1939.
J. B. Williamson, *The History of the Temple* [in London], London: John Murray, 1924, pp. 30–43.

The Templars: The Grail

Chrétien de Troyes, *The Complete Romances*, trans. D. Staines, Bloomington: University of Indiana Press, 1990.
Wolfram von Eschenbach, *Parzival*, trans. A. T. Hatto, London: Penguin, 1980.
Robert de Boron, *Joseph of Arimathea: A Romance of the Grail*, trans. J. Rogers, London: Rudolf Steiner Press, 1990.
The Quest of the Holy Grail, trans. P. M. Matarasso, London: Penguin, 1969.
P. M. Matarasso, *The Redemption of Chivalry*, Geneva: Droz, 1979.
H. J. Nicholson, *Love, War and the Grail: Templars, Hospitallers and Teutonic Knights in Medieval Epic and Romance*, Leiden: Brill, 2001.

For a survey:
R. Barber, *The Holy Grail: Imagination and Belief*, London: Penguin, 2004.

On the origins of the grail:
J. Goering, *The Virgin and the Grail: Origins of a Legend*,
   Yale University Press, 2005.

I have gratefully used the translations in:
Chrétien de Troyes, *The Complete Romances*, trans. D.
   Staines, Bloomington: University of Indiana Press, 1990.
Wolfram von Eschenbach, *Parzival*, trans. A. T. Hatto,
   London: Penguin, 1980.

The Templars: Suppression

The documents in:
J. Michelet, *Le Procès des Templiers*, Paris: Les Éditions du
   C.T.S.H., 1987.

A selection with French translation:
G. Lizerand (ed.), *Le Dossier de l'Affaire des Templiers*,
   Paris: H. Champion, 1923.

For a classic treatment:
M. Barber, *The Trial of the Templars*, Cambridge:
   Cambridge University Press, 1978.

On magic:
P. Partner, *The Murdered Magicians*, Oxford University
   Press, 1981.

On the guilt of the Templars:
J. Riley-Smith, 'Were the Templars guilty?', *Proceedings*,
   London: The St John Historical Society, 2002, pp. 9–26.

I have gratefully used the translations of some documents
in:
M. Barber and K. Bate (eds), *The Templars*, Manchester
   University Press, 2002.
P. Partner, *The Murdered Magicians*, Oxford University
   Press, 1981.

Notes for Further Reading

Constantine

On the Council of Nicaea and the Creed:
J. N. D. Kelly, *Early Christian Creeds*, London: A. & C. Black, 1972, pp. 205–62.

On Arius:
R. Williams, *Arius: Heresy and Tradition*, London: Darton, Longman & Todd, 1987.

On Constantine and Christianity:
R. Lane Fox, *Pagans and Christians*, London: Viking, 1986, pp. 609–62.

The Gnostics

Two classic surveys of Gnosticism:
H. Jonas, *The Gnostic Religion*, Boston: Beacon Press, 1963. (The Jewish Jonas had to flee Germany in the 1930s; his recognition of the social implications of Gnosticism is deep and moving.)
K. Rudolph, *Gnosis*, San Francisco: Harper, 1987.

Histories sympathetic to the epistemology of the Gnostics:
G. Filoramo, *A History of Gnosticism*, trans. A. Alcock, Oxford: Basil Blackwell, 1990.
K. L. King, *What is Gnosticism?*, Harvard University Press, 2003.

The Gospel of Thomas, and saying 114 in particular (the subject of a vast literature):
I have used the translation in A. Guillaumont *et al.*, *The Gospel According to Thomas*, Leiden: Brill, 1959.
A. Marjanen, 'Women disciples in the *Gospel of Thomas*', in R. Uro (ed.), *Thomas at the Crossroads*, Edinburgh: T. & T. Clark, 1998, pp. 89–106.

The Gospel of Philip:
A translation: J. M. Robinson (ed.), *The Nag Hammadi Library in English*, 3rd edn, Leiden: Brill, 1988, pp. 139–60.

An edition: R. Mc L. Wilson, *The Gospel of Philip*, London: A. R. Mowbray, 1962.

R. M. Grant, 'The mystery of marriage in the Gospel of Philip', *VC* 15, 1961, pp. 129–40.

J. J. Buckley, 'A cult-mystery in the Gospel of Philip', *JBL* 99, 1980, pp. 569–81.

E. Pagels, 'The mystery of marriage in the Gospel of Philip', in B. A. Pearson (ed.), *The Future of Early Christianity: FS Helmut Koester*, Minneapolis: Fortress, 1991, pp. 442–52.

E. Pagels, 'Ritual in the Gospel of Philip', in J. D. Turner and A. McGuire (eds), *Nag Hammadi Library after Fifty Years*, Leiden: Brill, 1997, pp. 280–94.

The Gospel of Mary:
Translation in: J. M. Robinson (ed.), *The Nag Hammadi Library in English*, 3rd edn, Leiden: Brill, 1988, pp. 523–7. (The Gospel of Mary was not among the texts found at Nag Hammadi.)

I have gratefully used the translation in W. Schneemelcher, *New Testament Apocrypha*, R. McL. Wilson (trans. and ed.), Cambridge: James Clarke, 1991, vol. I, pp. 391–5.

For the theme of these pages, see too the essays in: K. L. King (ed.), *Images of the Feminine in Gnosticism*, Harrisburg: Trinity, 1998.

Celibacy

The classic treatment on ascetic movements in early Christianity is:
P. Brown, *The Body and Society*, New York: Columbia University Press, 1988.

The Gospel of John and its Easter Story

For a fuller account:
R. Griffith-Jones, *The Four Witnesses*, San Francisco: Harper, 2000, pp. 342–77.

Also by Robin Griffith-Jones

The Four Witnesses: Why the Gospels Present Strikingly different Portraits of Jesus

A courageous exploration of the contrasting ways in which Jesus of Nazareth is depicted in the gospels. *The Four Witnesses* remains lucid, urgent and persuasive even as its author blazes his own trail through the thickets of bible scholarship.

The Los Angeles Times

The Four Witnesses offers a judicious, skilled and closely integrated analysis of the Christian gospels. The literary coloration of each gospel is dealt with in the light of the community and culture out of which it rose. The scholarship is impeccable, the style light of heart and hand.

The Revd Daniel Berrigan, SJ

In this lucid and engrossing book, Robin Griffith-Jones integrates the story of Jesus with the story of four very different first-century communities that would be fundamentally transformed by his life and teaching. Accessible, learned, and unfailingly interesting, *The Four Witnesses* is a wonderful introduction to the gospels and their setting.

Ron Hansen, author of Mariette in Ecstasy and Atticus

A remarkable achievement; quite apart from what you do with the gospels themselves, you manage to create a thoroughly credible historical setting for the whole of early Christianity.

The Rt Revd N. T. Wright

The Gospel According to Paul

This is the most helpful book on Paul I have ever read. I am deeply indebted to its author.

Prof Huston Smith, author of The World's Religions

One of the sharpest and most provocative readings of Paul that I have ever encountered. Robin manages to synthesize and build upon the most cutting edge studies in Pauline scholarship . . . His own argument is stunning and original and deeply informed about the Jewish mystical milieu of the apostle.

Prof Frances Flannery-Dailey, Hendrix University

Robin's next book, *Mary Magdalene: The Woman Whom Jesus Loved*, is published by Harper San Francisco, autumn 2007.